THE
NEW BIRTH
of
CHRISTIANITY

The New Birth of Christianity

Why Religion Persists in a Scientific Age

RICHARD A. NENNEMAN

HarperSanFrancisco

A Division of HarperCollins*Publishers*

FIRST EDITION

Library of Congress Cataloging-in-Publication Data

Nenneman, Richard A.
  The new birth of Christianity: why religion persists in a scientific age / Richard A. Nenneman.—1st ed.
     p.   cm.
  Includes bibliographical references.
  ISBN 0-06-250615-3 (alk. paper)
  1. Christian Science. 2. United States—Religion—1960–
I. Title.
BX6943.N39   1992
289.5—dc20   91-50501
                                                                      CIP

92 93 94 95 96 ❖ RRD(H) 10 9 8 7 6 5 4 3 2 1

This edition is printed on acid-free paper that meets the American National Standards Institute Z39.48 Standard.

CONTENTS

PREFACE

I WROTE THIS BOOK FOR THE REASONS GIVEN IN THE FIRST chapter. Because these reasons underlie the development of the chapters that follow, they were included as part of the book and not as a preface. I generally find that readers skip the preface.

For readers who do begin at the very beginning, however, this preface seems to be an appropriate place to state that I am not unaware of the environment in which I have written this book. While claiming that Christian Science can be looked at as an important articulation of Christian themes that have been present in Christianity since its inception, and particularly in claiming that Christian Science offers a way to spirituality, a desire for which is inherent to some degree in every person, I realize that recent court cases in several states of the United States have raised questions in the public mind about the practice of spiritual healing in Christian Science. In fact, if one were to draw conclusions regarding Christian Science from most of the media publicity given to these cases, he or she would hardly think that Christian Science lies as near the flow of mainstream Christianity as it does.

However, this short book is not written as a defense of spiritual healing nor in response to these recent cases. Rather, the development of the ideas in the pages that follow has gone on in my own thought for many years.

It is sometimes the case, when people adopt a new language, that they become so engrossed in its use that they are unaware that others are also adopting a new language—but not the one they have just learned themselves. Inadequate as this analogy may be, there is a similarity here to the world in which Christian Science attempts to make itself useful. Students of Christian Science work with a textbook, *Science and Health with Key to the Scriptures*, which Mary Baker Eddy first published in 1875 and to which she made revisions almost up until the time of her passing in 1910. Her articulation of Christianity in metaphysical terms has a language unique to her. Students of Christian Science find no difficulty in grasping the essential direction of her teachings. Those who are often working the most earnestly to become modern-day followers of Christ Jesus through their individual study and practice of Christian Science are understandably immersed in the vocabulary and the particular categorization of thought that Mrs. Eddy gave to Christian Science. And their spoken, or unspoken, hope often is "If others would only learn to use this too."

In the century since the Christian Science textbook was written, though, the "language" that one hears out of the other Christian churches has changed. Within many denominations, doctrinal matters are of less pressing importance today. Many of the mainline Protestant denominations have turned to an emphasis on social justice and a broad application of Christian moral principles to the body politic, while many of the more conservative branches of Christianity lay just as heavy an emphasis on the personal moral issues that confront every Christian. Catholics and Protestants alike have been challenged to look at the sources of the New Testament anew, as a result both of new texts that have come to light and of new historical methods of studying the old. To the degree that any of the historical emphases of Christianity have changed, whether in matters of doctrine or individual behavior, or because of the present conception of the physical universe that theoretical physicists entertain, one can say that the "language" of Christianity has also moved on during this momentous century.

These inevitable developments in the general culture do not make Christian Science out of date any more than they make Christianity out of date. But they do require anyone whose articulation of a particular point of view is in one language to make sure that it still resonates in the ears of those hearing it today—whose own "language," as it were, has been in swift evolution.

If I have successfully forged that connection in the pages that follow, this book will in fact make the reliance on spiritual healing that is a large and vital element of Christian Science a more understandable phenomenon. Even more important, though, it will make the concept of an active spirituality in all one's human affairs a challenge to be accepted by any person who is looking for deeper meaning in life.

I have benefited from the suggestions of several persons who read early drafts of this manuscript. In particular, I have appreciated the comments of Rev. William Fore and Prof. Elaine Pagels. Bill Fore, who is currently teaching at the Yale Divinity School, was for twenty years the director of communications for the National Council of Churches. If this book was an attempt to communicate where Christian Science stands vis-à-vis the historical Christian tradition, I needed to know if I was in fact communicating. Rev. Fore's reaction to the manuscript encouraged me to complete the effort. Elaine Pagels, who is head of the department of religion at Princeton University, is an outstanding authority on the gnostic movement, and was particularly helpful in reviewing chapter 4. In acknowledging my gratitude to both Rev. Fore and Prof. Pagels, I do not presume to imply that either of them agrees entirely with the positions I have taken.

EAST ORLEANS, MASSACHUSETTS
May 1991

Chapter 1

WHY RELIGION PERSISTS
IN A SCIENTIFIC AGE

Whatever names we may want to hang onto this century, this is certainly the age of science. The world approaches the end of a century of unparalleled scientific discovery and technological achievement. Yet neither the discoveries nor their remarkable applications touch the personal hunger most of us feel for meaning in our lives—for identification with something or someone bigger and more enduring than we sense our own mortal lives to be.

The Gospel of John relates how Nicodemus came to Jesus by night and asked what he had to do to find salvation. When Jesus told him he must be born again, Nicodemus took the message literally. He could not enter into his mother's womb again, he said. Then came Jesus' reply: "That which is born of the flesh is flesh; and that which is born of the Spirit is spirit."[1] While Christianity contains many elements, its core element of looking at and living life from a spiritual standpoint is its quintessence, underlying its ethical and moral imperatives of love and compassion for others.

This age-old Christian theme of being born again, of learning what it means to turn from reliance on the sense of life projected by the human mind and the five senses to a more spiritual outlook, is one of the themes of this small book. The other is an even older one that runs through the great epics of every age: man's search for a home. The themes are united by the fact that, in being born again, we come home.

That eminent mythologist, the late professor Joseph Campbell, often talked of an individual's life as setting forth on an adventure, at the end of which he hoped to reach home again. The great epics of literature are built around journeys—often physical journeys—that epitomize the individual's search for the values, roots, and comfort that characterize home. Stripped of all its superfluous doctrinal baggage, Christianity remains "home" for those of us who were raised in cultures that are still nominally Christian. While it proclaims itself a universal religion, Christianity should continue to have particular significance for those who were raised on a literature heavy with biblical allusions and in a political culture much of whose strength derives from the Jewish and Christian concepts of one universal God and man's equality before him.

Nothing that has happened in the physical sciences or in the newer mental discipline of psychology eclipses or replaces the mental and spiritual home people still find in the simple Christianity of Christ Jesus. Yet there is much in the culture of the late twentieth-century West—perhaps in Europe even more than in America—that has acted to deprive man of recognizing where home is.

Each of these themes—the new birth that Christianity both demands and provides, and the deep need most men and women feel for a sense of a mental and spiritual resting place, or home—finds a corresponding subtheme in this book, written by a Christian who also became, during his college years at Harvard, a Christian Scientist. For the author, a Christian rebirth came about through the study and practice of Christian Science. For many thousands, in fact, the home they sought in Christianity has come more clearly into view through the explanations given to the life and work of Christ Jesus, as well as to the dominant theological concepts of Christianity, in the teachings of Christian Science.

*   *   *

The New Testament tells the story of a man, Christ Jesus, who expressed unlimited dominion over material circumstance. He healed uncounted numbers of illness; he demonstrated a supply of food and wine where there was not enough; he walked on the water. And finally, he himself rose from the dead, after being crucified, and then rose above material apprehension entirely. He also taught an ethic of living that was based on a single word, love. He taught, in some of the direct teachings such as the Sermon on the Mount that have come down to us in the Gospels, that a life of service to others is the highest human good. Through enduring the passion experience, he demonstrated at one and the same time both his ethic of love and his understanding of true being (a perfect, indestructible, spiritual selfhood).

Now, if most of us thought we could achieve even a fraction of that kind of fulfilled living, as well as the dominion that Jesus showed, would we not give some time to trying to understand how this could be done? Most of Christianity, however, has become either weighted down with a system of beliefs, as opposed to practice, or reduced to an ethical system without spiritual force accompanying it. The result is that we look almost everywhere else for answers to life's meaning, and for more dominion over our own affairs, rather than turning to the Bible and the life of Christ Jesus. This is not to diminish the importance of what many of the Christian churches have done in addressing the need for social justice—for proper worker representation in economic decision making earlier in the twentieth century, or for often spearheading the civil rights movement in the past twenty years, or for their watchdog role over strict obedience to many constitutional safeguards. Yet the fact remains that the practice of Christianity in modern times has not been as closely linked with the control of one's own mental life, or as the basis for relationships with others, or with the establishment and maintenance of health so vividly portrayed in the works of Jesus and the Apostles.

In the United States especially, the control of one's individual mental balance and the management of a myriad of problems involving personal relationships have increasingly come to be seen as a field for psychology. The maintenance of physical well-being, on the other hand, is seen as largely the responsibility of the medical technicians. Today large numbers of people work from the premise that their own individual exercise and dietary habits have as much to do with health as what the doctors can do for them after they are sick; but whether it is self-induced health or a medical care system run by the doctors, health and the healing of illness itself are not generally looked upon as part of the exercise of Christianity.

Not only is the maintenance of physical and mental health seen as little connected with the practice of Christianity. Much of the impetus for looking into other cultures and religions, particularly in the Far East, comes from a belief that these other systems may be able to supply something lacking in the Judeo-Christian tradition. There is a positive side to this breakout from Western "provincialism," if that is the word for it; it indicates an awareness of other peoples and the fact that there has been more than one approach to finding meaning and comfort in life. The search is usually frustrated, however, because one cannot easily adapt to a system of thought that applies to a wholly different mental environment without some awareness of its cultural totality.

It is my concern that much of today's generation has already lost the words and symbols of both the Jewish Old Testament and the Christian New Testament. Even those symbols, without the practice of the religion, have served as a unifying force in Western life for two millennia. There is vastly more to Christianity than its symbols and particular vocabulary, of course, but even our ignorance of Shadrach, Meshach, and Abednego, or of the five foolish virgins, or of Paul's shipwreck as important Bible stories or parables is a sign of the degree to which biblical symbols have been eliminated from much of modern life.

In his 1987 best-seller, *The Closing of the American Mind*, Allan Bloom uses a relevant phrase: that ". . . the categories of the mind determine the perceptions." It is reminiscent of Ludwig Wittgenstein's phrase, "You see what you want to see." What we don't even think about we won't ever know. If we close out whole categories of life from investigation, they could just as well not exist for us. Bloom himself gives the example of a young person visiting paintings of the Old Masters in the Louvre or the Uffizi galleries.

> In his innocence of the stories of Biblical and Greek or Roman antiquity, Raphael, Leonardo, Michelangelo, Rembrandt and all the others can say nothing to him. All he sees are colors

and forms—modern art. In short, like almost everything else in his spiritual life, the paintings and statues are abstract.[2]

Those who originally saw such works of art—and this includes the ordinary person of those times—understood them. They evoked an inner reality that was there because of one's common cultural and religious heritage. "It is not merely the tradition that is lost when the voice of civilization elaborated over millennia has been stilled in this way. It is being itself that vanishes beyond the dissolving horizon."[3]

* * *

This book was conceived out of concern that too many people's view of life has indeed been narrowed or diminished. For me, as for others, Christian Science was the means of returning, coming home, to the underlying message in the life of Christ Jesus—for it is the example of his life that is needed today more than theories and doctrines *about* that life. A second purpose is also a coming home in a broader sense: to show that Christianity remains the key with which at least this Western civilization has approached the spiritual life for two millennia. In spite of new cosmologies of the universe, man needs a spiritual home. And no one is more aware of this than some of the world's leading theoretical physicists themselves. Moreover, when one has come to feel from experience that an explanation of the spiritual force that impelled the life of Jesus has more meaning for modern man than any of the psychological structures of the twentieth century or systems of religion that have served other cultures, he simply wants to share what he has found.

Almost anyone who might benefit from the study of Christian Science, as an avenue to practical daily Christianity, is totally unaware of that fact. And what sometimes appears as animosity toward Christian Science is more often than not the result of having no personal knowledge of the teachings of Christian Science, its practice, or its grounding in the mainstream of Christian history and tradition.

Even to make the statement that assumes a "benefit" from the study of something as serious and presumably God-connected as religion runs the risk of making Christian Science sound like one of the self-improvement fads so rampant in twentieth-century America. It is not! It is a religion as demanding as old-style Calvinism was. But it is a form of Christianity—and more than a form, a practice—that also includes the dominion that the master Christian, Christ Jesus, expressed in his daily round. Its study does bring to its students an increasing sense of dominion over their everyday experience. This dominion includes the healing of physical and mental illness; the maintenance of health; a desire, along with a growing ability, to live according to the moral and ethical commands of the Bible; freedom from fear; and, above all for most Christian Scientists, a sense of purpose and place in a modern world in which man has become increasingly one of the homeless—as assuredly as are the physically homeless in New York City who seek for shelter at night in the subterranean levels of Grand Central Station.

"Run the risk," I wrote, because one may at first assume that a person is drawn to a religion for the most altruistic of purposes—to know God, to drop at least somewhat the human for the divine. Yet, as the nineteenth-century philosopher and psychologist William James put it in *The Varieties of Religious Experience*, men most often come to religion out of self-interest. They want something that makes sense of their place in the universe.

To most of us, nothing is as central as our own development, growth, and progress. In fact, the starting point of a life of altruism or even sacrifice may apparently be selfish. James wrote:

> The pivot round which the religious life, as we have traced it, revolves, is the interest of the individual in his private personal destiny. Religion, in short, is a monumental chapter in the history of human egotism. . . . To-day, quite as much as at any previous age, the religious individual tells you that the divine meets him on the basis of his personal concerns.[4]

We may learn that our own happiness or health can be found only as we define our lives in relation to other human beings, or as we find a source outside ourselves that endows us with a degree of physical, mental, and spiritual strength beyond what we could summon without that connection we feel with the divine.

James was well aware of the conceptual challenge that advancing knowledge in the physical sciences presented to traditional religion at the end of the nineteenth century—the very decades in which Christian Science was becoming established in the United States. In fact, the juxtaposition of his own writing with the period when this new religion was gaining recognition is one factor that makes his views on religion so relevant to this book. One by one, the sciences seemed to be constricting the domain of scholastic religion. If God had made the universe, it was at best a God "of universal laws exclusively, a God who does a wholesale, not a retail business," James wrote. Once upon a time, not too many generations before this, "whatever you imagined in a lively manner, whatever you thought fit to be true, you affirmed confidently; and whatever you affirmed, your comrades believed. Truth was what had not yet been contradicted."[5]

Although James would have agreed with the scientific search for facts—for truth—and did not mourn the demise of those religious beliefs that the sciences seemed to contradict irrefutably, it did not follow at all that he saw the demise of religion. In fact, the very impersonality of the sciences, their appeal to universal, nonpersonal laws, left a void in terms of the individual's understanding of his place in the universe. "So long as we deal with the cosmic and the general," he wrote, "we deal only with the symbols of reality, but as soon as we deal with private and personal phenomena as such, we deal with realities in the completest sense of the term."[6]

What man can think about may be cosmic in scope. The recently completed (1989) odyssey of Voyager II to all the known planets of our solar system, with its magnificent pictures of Neptune and its moon, Triton, suggests the physical scope of what man can conceive. And beyond the planets, we know there is a vaster physical universe awaiting our further knowledge. Yet, the only reality we actually perceive, day in and day out, is the reality of what goes on in the individual consciousness. Again, James:

> That unsharable feeling which each one of us has of the pinch of
> his individual destiny as he privately feels it rolling out of fortune's
> wheel may be disparaged for its egotism, may be sneered at as

unscientific, but it is the one thing that fills up the measure of our concrete actuality.[7]

James concluded that, because religion concerned itself with "personal destinies and keeping thus in contact with the only absolute realities which we know," it would play a permanent role in the history of mankind. This does not plant religion on the absolute grounds on which the world's religious leaders would place it. Nor does it address the question of whether religion deals primarily with a set of universal ethics and a moral code by which man can live with his fellowman in peace and harmony, or whether religion must also claim a transcendent vision of man's relation to the universe. However, by differentiating between the objectivity and impersonality of the world of the theoretical physicists and the actuality centered around each person looking out at his own world, one can understand the persistence of the religious impulse.

The religious search begins for most, not because they are looking for God, but because they want a better life. James quotes another professor of his day thus:

> Does God really exist? How does he exist? What is he? are so many irrelevant questions. Not God, but life, more life, a larger, richer, more satisfying life, is, in the last analysis, the end of religion. The love of life at any and every level of development, is the religious impulse.[8]

This may sound like a strange introduction to a religion whose greatest Exemplar taught that to sacrifice one's life for others was the greatest end of man. Yet Jesus himself also taught, "I am come that ye might have life, and that ye might have it more abundantly."[9]

* * *

The continuing pages of this book attempt to show the relevance of Jesus' Christianity to today's world, and particularly to illustrate the strong connection between Christian Science and the teachings of Jesus. Chapter 2 deals with a dilemma posed by today's world, particularly as seen by those with a Christian background. It will discuss the decline of traditional organized religion, at least as measured by social scientists, along with evidence that large numbers of people are looking for new guideposts by which to live, including a deeper spirituality in their own approach to life. It will discuss the traditional dilemma Christians have faced of being *in* the world but not *of* the world. In this chapter, as in several others, we will introduce, where relevant, something of the position of Christian Science, while reserving the main explanation of Christian Science to chapters 7 and 8. There is a necessary background to be filled in before one arrives at the point where Mary Baker Eddy stood when she began to articulate the metaphysical system of Christian Science and its practice. There have already been too many cursory attempts to explain the language of Christian Science without the cultural and mental context within which it was brought to light or without an appreciation for the deep Christian motivation behind Mrs. Eddy's work.

Chapter 3 discusses the effect of modern science on a revealed religion such as Christianity. Have the most current theories of the theoretical physicists further dethroned the insights of revealed religion—or have they actually presented an opening for them? This chapter attempts to show how Christian Science, viewing itself as scientific, looks at the world of physical reality and the theories underlying theoretical research today. It also looks briefly at Darwin and Freud, whose researches in biology and the life of the mind account for much of the popular mind-set of the twentieth century.

Then, before proceeding to some basic positions of Christian Science and their relation to the life and work of Christ Jesus, it is necessary to pick up two other threads that are woven into this discussion. The first (chapter 4) is to remind ourselves how, as one writer puts it, "the kingdom of God became Christianity."[10] From the time of Jesus, with his simple hillside sermons, to the creeds about him some three hundred years later, there was considerable development in thinking about what his life meant and who he was. Some knowledge of this is necessary to appreciate what Mrs. Eddy set out to do in what she called the restoration of primitive Christianity.

We will also look in some detail at several elements in the early Christian movement that came to be discredited in later centuries by the bishops. As the Church became more organized, acceptance of certain doctrinal points and obedience to an ecclesiastical structure became the definition of "Christian." It is possible that some of the views of those who were eventually labeled heretics, such as the loosely knit gnostic movement, were closer in spirit to primitive Christianity than some of the views that prevailed later. This is not to say that the gnostics were generally right and the orthodox church wrong. The gnostics did raise serious issues, however, and their heresy throws more light on the basic questions the early Church tried to answer than does perhaps any other single movement.

The other issue, to be raised in chapter 5, is the nature of discovery. Christian Science is referred to, by its adherents, as a discovery, and Mary Baker Eddy as both its discoverer and founder. At the same time, it claims to be a return to original Christianity. To call Christian Science a discovery is to claim, in effect, an identity with original Christianity. It is to say that it has existed, but not been recognized, since the time of Jesus and his apostles. Why are discoveries generally made by individuals? Why do at least some discoveries take a long period of time before they are adopted by the very people who would get the most benefit from them?

After these issues are discussed, the reader will be in a better position to deal with the discovery of Christian Science, with some of its basic tenets, and finally with the concept of *practice* in Christian Science. This will be done through three separate chapters—one dealing with the early American and then the immediate nineteenth-century background of Mary Baker Eddy; one discussing the theological points that most curious people would probably raise about Christian Science; and one explaining the practice of Christian Science. The practice is a difficult concept to talk about in abstract. To much of the public, it seems to mean doing without doctors. To the Christian Scientist, the practice is in one sense the whole of his life. If one is a serious student of Science, he is trying to apply its metaphysics to the regeneration of every aspect of his daily living and to find God's guidance in every decision he makes. Handling physical or mental ills is only one aspect of living and, for most lifelong students of Christian Science, not the kind of "practice" they engage in most frequently. The closest analogy may be to say that a Christian Scientist looks on all of his life holistically; but that term has connotations that are not entirely in line with the metaphysics of Christian Science. In any case, while no one actually learns to swim without getting in the water, the attempt is made in this chapter to learn what the practice means—but out of water!

There is a summary nature to all the material in this book, which I prefer to think of, in its entirety, as a long introductory essay to a vast subject. Any single chapter could become a book of its own. The chapters on modern science and the early Church do not treat their subjects in a thoroughgoing manner; their main purpose is to prepare the background for what follows. I have, of course, tried to be objective in the limited treatment given to the subjects selected. One can appreciate, in particular, the valiant attempts the theologians of the early Church made to deal with the person of Christ Jesus. They were close enough to the event to feel its impact on the world, and they believed that, with Jesus' advent, a different kind of light had come to illumine the world and that a new authority had been introduced into human affairs.

This book does not cover the Church of the Middle Ages or the Reformation at all, since it is not an essay on religious history. In omitting the centuries in between, however, there needs to be at least the comment that this does not in any way detract from the author's own appreciation for the civilizing role the Church played in the Middle Ages or its even more important role in keeping alive the ancient Bible texts until the ages were ready for a new appraisal of them.

✳   ✳   ✳

The material in the next few chapters covers several subjects, going from a discussion of concepts of reality to the "old theology" debated in the early centuries of Christianity. Not all the terminology may be familiar, but it is no more difficult to understand than discussions of politics or psychotherapy in the Sunday magazines.

Most of us, in our professional lives, deal with matters of some complexity. To use an example having a very large common denominator today, the computer has entered into our experience in a way that demands much more knowledge than operating a typewriter ever did. The entire structure of business and scientific organizations is being changed by the use of interactive computers, by the availability of relevant intelligence on a more timely basis. We are not all computer hacks, but most computer users are challenged to dig deeper into their manuals if they want to make the best use of this most innovative tool in terms of changing the way work is accomplished. Most of us rise to meet that challenge because we see that the results are well worth the additional effort.

If you have got this far, my hope is that you will feel a few hours' extra effort is worth it to see how Christian Science fills the needs with which we began this chapter—an understanding of what Jesus meant when he told Nicodemus of the necessity of being born again, and how that new birth does bring us home to that inner place of spiritual peace where we can gather the strength, intelligence, and grace to meet life's challenges.

Chapter 2

AMERICANS AND THEIR RELIGIOUS BELIEFS AND PRACTICES AT THE CLOSE OF THE TWENTIETH CENTURY

A century after William James said that the religious impulse endures would seem to be time enough to have tested his claim. Certainly there has been no other century in the history of mankind in which the outward circumstances of daily living have changed so drastically. In the developed world, millions of people live in material circumstances that only the very wealthy enjoyed a few centuries ago. The varieties of food we can easily purchase, the fashionable clothes people wear, the cars they drive, the vacations they can take almost anywhere in the world—all are evidence of a life-style that would not have been dreamed of a century ago. Instant communications and what amounts to near-instant travel are changing the way we look at and experience the rest of the world. Scientific research and its application in technology continue to shrink the areas of the unknown, but at the same time to reveal a mysteriously wonderful universe.

Yet religion endures. Scientific progress has, in fact, brought about a revival of various kinds of religious fundamentalism, in part as a reaction to the rate of change and the deadening superficiality of much of modern life. In this chapter we shall try to assess the strength of religion today, to ask whether or not common measures of religious interest indicate a genuine search for spirituality, and to see on what "terms," so to speak, people want to come to church today.

Finally, because this book deals with the subject of the new birth and because the trend in American Protestantism today is toward the evangelical churches, we shall see where Christian Science places itself in the spectrum of the "new born" or "born again" Christians, as well as in a related measure common to Christian discussion, the world-liness or lack thereof of Christians.

* * *

CHALLENGES TO A SPIRITUAL OUTLOOK

The secularization of late twentieth-century life has certainly altered any approach to a discussion of religion from what it would have been one hundred years ago. Whatever obstacles Mary Baker Eddy found in her way, in preaching and practicing a new form of Christianity, she did not have to convince the public of the impor-tance of religion.

In the first part of this chapter, we shall discuss what one means by the secularization of life, noting that it is the culmination of a pro-cess that actually began with the end of the religious wars in the sev-enteenth century. We will then look at some current sociological data on the professed beliefs and church habits of Americans today. In some ways, these argue against a secularization theory, until one asks whether stated beliefs, or even presence in church on Sunday, are not actually phenomena that might coexist readily with the secular life. If by Christianity one means an approach to life that is in many respects at variance with the life-style and unspoken assump-tions of the secular society, if Christianity still means that one has in some way been born again, there seems little question that a more secular view of life is now dominant.

The decline of the church as an institution of the first rank and the decline of individual religious commitment and values are not identical. Some people today maintain, in fact, that they can carry out their religious values better without the encumbrance of an imperfect institutional church in their lives. Yet, by and large, it is safe to assume, at least in Western societies, that the presence of an organized church has acted to preserve and promote moral and spiritual values that would be substantially less in evidence without the church. Thus the decline of the church as an institution would be synonymous with some loss of attention to religious values in a society as a whole.

Many factors have contributed to this institutional decline—both in North America and in Europe, where the decline began earlier. Some observers go all the way back to the Thirty Years' War (1618–1648), the last of the major wars fought over the Protestant Reformation. By the middle of the seventeenth century, many European intellectuals and members of the upper classes had grown tired of religious rivalry and of the misdeeds perpetrated in the name of religion.

While religious thought still had a major role to play in the private lives of most people, Christianity as an institutional force in Western society had lost the prime position it had occupied for over one thousand years. Nor was it only religious bickering that caused the gradual decline of organized Christianity. The rise of a new age of scientific rationalism came to claim the first allegiance of Europe's intellectuals—both scientists and philosophers. New scientific knowledge successfully challenged much of the cosmological view that had long been an integral part of orthodox Christianity.

When Friedrich Nietzsche, in his prolific decade of writing in the 1880s, published book after book criticizing Christianity, he was articulating what was already in the public thought. Nietzsche pictured religion, and particularly Christianity, as a negative influence in man's development. The aggressive tone of his writing, which was not helped by its obscurity, did not make him a cult hero at the time. In the following decades, however, his influence became immense in intellectual circles, particularly in Europe. The experience of two devastating wars for Europe, and the need after each one to concentrate on the externalities of life, did not favor the extension of the influence of organized religion.

In America, one must speak of the decline of the influence of organized religion rather than of the churches themselves. In fact, in some Protestant denominations, church membership continues to grow today. The phenomenon of religious pluralism that developed early in American life has a good deal to do with explaining this. While much of Western Europe had mainly the Roman Catholic church and one leading Protestant confession, America had them all—simply because the United States had been settled by immigrants from all the countries of Europe.

Early New England tried to maintain a parish church, to which all the members of a community belonged. Contrary to what many evangelical Christians think today, the early Puritan church was not a confessional kind of church. That is, one did not have to have a conversion experience to become a member. (This came some hundred years later, at the time of Jonathan Edwards and the Great Awakening.) One was a member simply by virtue of being born into the community.

To the early Puritans, who believed in the doctrine of predestination (under which only a minority of us could be "saved"), it was unthinkable that the church elders should themselves be in a position to know who had received this saving grace. Thus, while the doctrine of predestination had its ugly side, in denying even the possibility of universal salvation, its believers did not themselves try to make the judgment that belonged to God alone. Had they made this judgment, the parish church could not have existed.

As it was, such a church lasted for only a century or less in New England. Immigrants from other countries brought with them competing religious traditions. Moreover, church life on the frontier, whether the frontier was western Massachusetts or Ohio one hundred years later, was different from church life in settled New England villages. American religion, at least in the Protestant denominations, developed with the church as, among other things, a community function. Not everyone belonged to the same church, but every church became a center for communal activity.

If the intellect was less important in many denominations than it was to the relatively well educated early generations of Puritan theologians, a religion of the heart continued to meet many of the needs of successive generations of Americans. These needs may not all have been concerned with ultimate religious ends. The church nonetheless played a positive and vital role in the life of the majority of Americans well beyond the time it had ceased to function that way in much of Europe.

The biggest change in churchgoing habits in America has come in the past thirty years. (Two recent polls referred to later in this chapter somewhat dispute this contention. The Gallup poll, which covers a fifty-year span, notes an increase in public interest in religion in the 1950s.) After the Second World War, a generation of Americans wanted to forget both the war and the Depression that preceded it; they wanted to establish the outward symbols of stable living once again, and the church was one such symbol. A popular president, Dwight Eisenhower, encouraged church attendance. The fifties were a decade of substantial increase in churchgoing and church membership. The content of that activity is another matter; but the facade looked stronger than ever.

Since the 1950s, we have been witnessing the most rapid social change the nation has ever experienced. Much of this change has been positive:

- the civil rights movement; this has broadened into a wider societal concern for the implementation of the full legal rights of all racial and social minorities;
- the continued move not only toward full equality for women in the workplace (a part of the civil rights agenda), but for a broader response to the feminist agenda and its honest appraisal by both sexes;
- with a generalized prosperity for the last forty years, as well as the advent of the two-worker family, the opening of many career options that belie the notion that Americans only worship material success;
- acceptance of the need to prudently balance the continued demand for economic growth with protection of the environment and a less drastic call on nonrenewable natural resources.

These positive developments have been accompanied, however, by a series of negative ones:

- Vietnam, the feeling that our government had gotten its people into the wrong war and couldn't say so;

- the first oil crisis in 1973, which was also the first awakening for many Americans to their vulnerability to the rest of the world;
- Watergate, which epitomized a growing doubt about the quality of American political leadership;
- a spreading drug and crime culture;
- a failed "war" on poverty and the further breakdown of families in a large subculture of America;
- the growth of a generation of young people who had few models to look up to in public life and who turned increasingly to personal pursuits, worthy or otherwise.

Although Vietnam and Watergate created doubts about the nature of America's leadership, it must be noted that the just-concluded short war to liberate Kuwait may have gone a long way toward erasing these older causes of negativism about Washington. It depends largely on the degree to which a continuing effort is made to eliminate the causes of instability in the Middle East and on the acumen that an American administration brings to that effort. Nor are American efforts alone going to be sufficient. However, the immediate reaction to the Kuwait liberation was caused not only by the fact that the war was such a successful operation; it was also seen as a validation of the proper use of American power.

Most of us are already familiar with the signposts, positive and negative, of the past generation. But another, deeper development has been going on for much longer, and it explains even more of the reason for the diminished position religion holds in life today. It is well articulated by an English author, Os Guinness, in a 1983 book, *The Gravedigger File.* Guinness suggests that the church's influence has been weakened by three simultaneous forces acting upon society: secularization, privatization, and pluralism. His excellent analysis is worthy of summary here.

Secularization

If one goes back to medieval times, when the spires of the church pierced the sky above the town and surrounding countryside, as at

Chartes, it had the highest position, and everything in life was defined in terms of its religious purpose. Guinness writes:

> [In the past] the deepest experiences of all were held to be "religious," "sacred," "other" or "transcendent," however these terms were defined. These experiences called ordinary life into question and cast a religious frame of meaning around the everyday world. Pursuits as down-to-earth as business deals, making love, farming and politics were all seen in the light of the world beyond. Human worlds had to creep in for shelter under the shade of divine truth.[1]

Guinness separates his word "secularization" from the philosophical word *secularism.* The latter is a philosophy. Agree with it or not, it is a position consciously held. It takes at least minimal effort. Secularization, on the other hand, is basically a process. It comes, as Carl Sandburg said of the fog, "on little cat feet." It describes the process of modernization that has crept over the Western world for at least two hundred years and eroded the sphere of religious influence in daily life.

> It comes as part and parcel of objective, institutional changes which have actually occurred through modernization and cannot be avoided or simply wished away. Secularization is therefore contagious in a way that secularism never is. Wherever modernization goes, some degree of infection is inevitable.[2]

This is perhaps best seen in the spread of Western, or modern, culture to the rest of the world. One of the reasons it has been resisted in a few countries has been that, coming as it did within a single generation, its effect on existing cultural patterns and religious institutions was more clearly discerned—and rejected. Iran is only an extreme example of the questioning going on in much of the Islamic world today. Most Islamic nations want to progress but do not know how to deal with the secularization that seems an inevitable part of a combination of modern technology and Western business organization.

In the West, the secularized society crept up on us in tiny bits, and for most people it was seen as a blessing. The "social and cultural significance of religion in the central areas of society, such as the worlds of science, technology, bureaucracy and so on" have been "neutralized," Guinness claims, by the gradual spread of these newer institutions and the mode of thought they represent. One can see in the spread of the scientific method, especially its insistence on objectivity and measurement, and the business system represented by the large corporation, the dominant mode of thought and the dominant institution in modern society.

Privatization

One result of the secularization of modern living has been to separate public and private activity. The demand for increased productivity in the factory (even if organized along modern work-group lines such as used by Volvo in Sweden) imposes a high degree of conformity on the workers. The schedule of a large office makes similar demands and builds a work ethic of the office. The need for the owners of a corporation to increase capital at regular intervals and in respectable amounts (that is, to remain competitive with other businesses using outside capital) puts a particular burden on its management. One's private life is fortunately still his own, but one too often finds his religion confined (according to Guinness) to that private sphere.

This is not always the case, of course, but in general it is an apt description. Those who take their ethical system to work with them may have to pay a price if it runs into conflicts with the workplace. I know the former vice president of a major New England bank who refused to approve a large loan he believed to be unsound. The president of the bank wanted the loan made, and it became a question of the vice president's integrity or his job. He chose to leave the bank. Not everyone is strong enough to make that choice. In many situations the practice of one's religion at the very least does not receive undue encouragement from the current ethics of the marketplace.

Relegating religion to one's private life would be all right if religion had no meaning beyond one's own beliefs. But if it is seen as the inner springboard from which all of one's actions take off, including the decisions made in the workplace and relationships with the rest of society, it would be meaningless to say that religion is only a private matter. If the practice of religion in America had indeed been only a private matter, how would the civil rights movement, which largely began in the churches, have become the major political issue it did in the 1960s?

The privatization of religion does provide greater freedom of religion. There are probably many forms of philosophy or systems of thought that do not function as recognized churches—at least to the extent of having a big edifice on some street corner. Having some interest in such systems is easier when one is not required to make full public disclosure of his interest. This generation may not realize how conformist American thought was on the subject of religion only a few generations ago. Severin Simonsen, a Methodist minister who became a Christian Science practitioner around the turn of this century, tells of his own healing in Christian Science in the late 1890s. He had been in declining health for many months, and doctors expected his illness to be terminal. When he finally decided to visit a Christian Science practitioner, he hoped no one would see him entering or leaving her house. In a generation when private persons can do just about anything they want without overt social judgment on them, this is hard to appreciate. (The more important part of the Simonsen story is that he went home unimpressed with the practitioner. They had simply talked for about twenty minutes, and he had expected something more. Perhaps his state of thought was analogous to Naaman's reaction on being told to wash in the Jordan River seven times! There was more! Within a few days Simonsen realized he had already been healed in that one brief visit.)[3]

So, privatization has probably increased the willingness to explore unpopular religions. That is not a negligible gain, if it has been bought for a small price. The price, however, is that privatization has reduced the institutional presence of religion. If religion in the end is only a question of man's relationship to God—however one defines God—what does the institutional presence matter? Is it not perhaps a barrier in some cases between man and God? What such an attitude ignores is that the nurturing of man's higher nature—the commitment to following one's highest sense of ethics and morality, concern for one's less fortunate neighbors, the need in organized society to tame the passions—is not the assignment of the public schools, nor is it the assignment of a local, state, or federal government.

The nurturing role of religion is, in the end, one that only the church and the family, standing apart from the aims of society as expressed in its political institutions, can provide. And the family needs all the help it can get today; it is unlikely to provide the ethical and moral guidance that children need if there isn't some support from the church in this direction. One's local church may not be a perfect institution. Looked at from an overall societal point of view, however, no other institution can take the place of the church. As Guinness correctly notes, the family and the church have been "the two strongest supports which traditionally undergirded people's private lives and tied them into a wider public world."[4]

Pluralization

Just as privatization helped the cause of religious freedom but at the same time undermined the church as one of the institutional pillars of society, pluralization has had a similar effect. It has made accessible ideas that might have taken much longer to get a hearing in a more structured society. However, it has placed into competition the most serious religious commitment one can make—a commitment that will fully work itself out only over an individual's entire life—with a myriad of vastly less important matters, such as the latest psychological fads, or the ways to a more fulfilling sex life, a healthier diet, or a better exercise system. What these "systems" have in common is that they compete for our time and thought within that limited private sector of our lives. It becomes ever more difficult for most people to sort out what is most important or to block out of thought and attention the systems in which they have no interest.

Even worse, the competition of ideas for our attention can tend to trivialize all ideas. Moreover, notes Guinness, "the extension of choice leads to the evasion of choice."[5] This, of course, is the risk one takes in a free society. If enough individuals fail to exercise their independent right to unfettered but informed thinking, their free society can be overtaken by mass movements that in the end are detrimental to their own freedom.

This picture of the secularization of life today does not appear overdrawn to me. It finds an echo in an even newer book (1989) by Rabbi Harold Kushner, *Who Needs God*. Addressing the absence of God in many people's lives, Kushner writes:

> Technology is the enemy of reverence. Deliberately or inadvertently technology puts out sacred fires because technology is the celebration of what man can do. . . . Ultimately the worship of man and the celebration of the man-made become boring precisely because it cannot lift us beyond ourselves. There is something in us that intuitively understands this.[6]

With this picture of secularization in mind, let us look at the rather amazing evidence of the continuity of religious patterns in American life. If these patterns are less disturbed on the surface than they actually are when one probes deeper into the meaning behind them, it is fortunate that the patterns are still as strong as they are. For, if Rabbi Kushner is right, that "something" in us that asks, in the songwriter's words, "Is That All There Is?" is still waiting to respond to the news that there is more.

Measures of Religious Interest Today

Current data on the "standing" of religion in American life actually show remarkable stability. Before looking briefly at some recent statistics, however, one should remind oneself that these compose a kind of sociological tableau of religious life. They do not probe deeply into what answers to certain questions really mean when applied to an individual's daily life. Moreover, some of the questions deal more with institutional standards, such as church attendance, than with the state of the person's innermost thoughts. But one would hardly expect any statistical sampling to have that ability in any case.

Two current books on the state of religious life in America provide abundant data. One, *The People's Religion: American Faith in the*

90's, by George Gallup, Jr., and Jim Castelli, summarizes data gathered by the Gallup organization. The other, by Andrew Greeley, a Roman Catholic priest, is *Religious Change in America*.

The Gallup survey covered the longer period. It found that 42 percent of Americans attend church weekly, compared with 41 percent fifty years ago. In the intervening years there have been both ups and downs: a low of 37 percent in 1940, a high of 49 percent during the Eisenhower years when America was trying to recapture, somewhat artificially, the image of its past (but also, positively, to get beyond the turmoil of both the Depression and the Second World War years).

Church membership has dropped somewhat during the fifty-year period, from 73 percent to the high sixties. However, this relatively small shift could be the result of the increased mobility of the nation's population as much as any other factor. Also, the two studies showed that churchgoing to some extent follows a life-cycle pattern. After the age of twenty-five, as more people marry and have families, they think more of the symbols of stability in their lives, as well as of the moral and ethical instruction the church should provide their children. The United States is now going through the maturing of the postwar baby boom which, if historical patterns hold, will bring more families back into churches in the next few years.[7]

The Greeley study largely confirmed the Gallup figures. Greeley's numbers are based on a thirty-year comparison. They show Protestant church attendance almost stable, at 44 percent in 1958 and 45 percent in 1985. Roman Catholic attendance was off the most, from 74 percent in 1958 to 48 percent in 1988. Greeley attributed this primarily to Catholics' discomfort with their church's continued opposition to normal family-planning methods.[8]

But what did the American public, churchgoing or not, believe at the end of the 1980s? According to Gallup,

- Ninety-four percent believe in God.
- Ninety percent say they pray.
- Eighty percent believe that God performs miracles.
- Seventy percent believe in life after death.

Gallup concluded that American society is unique in having a large percentage of the population that is both well educated and church-going. This is one of the historical differences between America and Europe, as noted at the start of this chapter. The question one must ask, though, is how deeply the beliefs people say they hold actually affect their daily lives. Anecdotal experience in my own life is necessarily limited to one individual's observations. It is my strong impression, however, that the description given by the Englishman Guinness of the state of religion in the West is very largely applicable to society as I have been seeing it as an adult for the past generation. The questions one would like to have answered are: What does this God mean to people who say they pray? What do they expect their prayers to accomplish? If God performs miracles, do they expect one in their own lives? As for life after death, it has been an eternal hope since man was first aware of his mortality. But is this hope, or even belief, strongly enough based to have an impact on how the individual who holds it lives his life while he still pays taxes every year?

Americans still have a place for church as an organization and for religious values in their lives. These values tend to relate to ethical and moral issues more than to spirituality as such. In fact, "spiritual" is a relatively vague word today, but it is certainly not passé. For instance, Gallup says that "a large majority believes the churches are too concerned with internal organizational issues and not sufficiently concerned with spiritual matters."[9]

What one means by "ethical and moral" is clearer. Some of the churches have taken a leadership role in fighting for civil rights and minority issues, in questioning the arms race, and in criticizing American policy toward smaller countries. These are important issues to churchgoing Americans and seen as the proper domain of religious concern—but not the boundary of religious concern.

Greeley writes convincingly that it is too simplistic to say that there is an American civil religion, that people go to church or say they believe something simply because others do. "[The civil religion theory] reduces American religion to an explanation which demands a day-or-night choice: either American religion is authentic, prophetic, and challenging or it is inauthentic, culture-supporting, and comforting. . . . In as large and complex a society as the US, both dimensions of religion almost certainly coexist both in their pure forms and in many admixtures of the two."[10]

Americans have little reason not to belong to a church, Greeley argues. Unlike societies in which an established church was part of the yoke that had to be thrown off, "religion in America has never been identified with any particular side in class struggles."

> If religion is about believing and belonging, if it provides a community to which people can belong and find explanation and reinforcement for the ultimate values (symbols) they share with other members of that community, then there is little in American experience to persuade most Americans that they should avoid such community and much to persuade them that they should join and be active in religious communities."[11]

This is not to say, nor would Greeley say, that such religious activity is ingenuous or insincere on the participant's part. However, there is also much evidence to the effect that the American ideal of individual freedom overrides most religious viewpoints. At the end of the line, one finds fewer and fewer people who would, in the German theologian Dietrich Bonhoeffer's words, submit their lives to Christ in the sense that he did. Quoting some words of Martin Luther's, Bonhoeffer ended a sermon on discipleship:

> Discipleship is not limited to what you can comprehend—it must transcend all comprehension. Plunge into the deep waters beyond your own comprehension, and I will help you to comprehend even as I do.[12]

That submission is not necessarily over the same issue; he was willing to die under the Nazis if it would help free Germany from the human degradation Hitler brought to his country. The American ideal of freedom is so deep that the general belief is that each of us controls his or her own life and makes the ultimate decisions. As a political statement, that is one thing; as religion, it puts a different cast on the relationship one thinks he or she has with God.

This helps explain some of the discrepancies in the current data. Gallup found, for instance, that eight in ten Americans believe they will stand before God on Judgment Day. Sixty-two percent say they believe that Christ Jesus will physically return to earth. "Such a nation," says Gallup, "cannot by any stretch of the imagination be described as secular in its core beliefs." Yet these same Americans, by a ratio of 45 to 36, say they rely on themselves to solve their problems rather than an outside power. They "tend to view their churches less as sources of faith than as resources for their personal and family religious and spiritual needs."[13] And Greeley says that American Catholics' "acceptance of papal authority" has declined; that many if not most Catholics, for instance, make their own decisions in matters of family planning but still consider themselves good Catholics.[14] This independence of attitude brings to mind Freud's mistaken belief that it wouldn't matter too much what the Americans did with psychoanalysis, since he did not take this country very seriously. Truth may not change color according to the climate, as a French essayist once claimed, but the American ethos does overlap if not actually infiltrate much of what it touches. (In chapter 6 we shall see how some of the elements of the American experience prepared the way for Mrs. Eddy's discovery.)

So, Americans do take their religion seriously; it is not merely a civil religion. At the same time, they also tend to come to it somewhat on their own terms. In the long run, this attitude would, at the very least, tend to dilute the kind of total commitment that orthodox Christianity demanded and that, in a different context, Christian Science requires for its successful practice. (The difference in the case of Christian Science, as later chapters will amplify, is that the mere acceptance of belief itself is of little importance. Normal measures of religious interest such as church attendance are of only somewhat more importance, while the concept of practice, which involves virtually all of one's activities, becomes the essence of being a Christian Scientist.) However, given the history of what now appear to have been religious delusions and excesses in the past, one can well understand how the present situation of coming to religion on one's own terms evolved.

Gallup says that those Americans who claim religion to be very important in their lives have dropped from a high of 75 percent in 1952 to about 55 percent today.[15] Thus, the answers to the various theological questions can be seen as being both entirely sincere but not necessarily affecting the decisions made on the job each day.

It would appear that the shrinking of the serious religious content in many people's lives has been due to the greater meaning they derive from other activities or lines of thought. Or, that their horizon has been so narrowed by the predominance of a materialistic view of life that there is not even an awareness of what is missing. In some cases, church attendance is also involved with community support, or even with coffee in the lounge after church.

The search for greater meaning or fulfillment in one's religion is also a partial explanation of the shifting allegiances among the churches. If present trends continue, Gallup claims that within the next generation a majority of Protestant church membership will be among the evangelical churches (where it is 45 percent today), and the nation will become even more pluralistic. This tendency will express itself in the growth of non-Western religions and in those who say they have no religion.[16]

That there still is a yearning for spirituality is evident from the kinds of activities going on outside the churches. In the winter of 1988, the British Broadcasting Corporation did a radio documentary on the upsurge in spirituality—"with more and more people going on retreat, with courses on prayer over-subscribed, with books on spirituality being best-sellers."

The head of religious broadcasting at the BBC wrote:

> As the media looks out at a world apparently tearing itself apart, more and more people appear to be looking in, seeking to harmonise their own personalities and experience of life with the will and purpose of God. In the noisiest society the world has ever known, people are creating whirlpools of silence."

Within just a few days of the broadcast, the BBC had close to a thousand requests for more information. "This gives the lie to two popular myths," the broadcaster said. "The first is that people today have outgrown religion. The second is that modern religion is all about sociology and politics. It isn't, of course. More and more it is, quite simply, about God."[17]

Secularization has indeed taken its toll. Whatever its obvious benefits in freeing thought from rigid but outmoded patterns, it has effectively squeezed the realm of the spiritual for millions of people. Yet not all that is modern is the result of secularization; much of what has happened in terms of technology, the organization of society, and human relations is actually the result of people's religion being put into practice both individually and corporately. And, as James showed one hundred years ago, the sciences themselves can never occupy the place or answer the questions for which we human beings come to religion.

THE NEW BIRTH; BORN-AGAIN CHRISTIANS

One thesis of this book is that mankind has a yearning for spirituality, however much that yearning may seem to be momentarily hidden or suppressed in many people. The "busyness" of modern society has indeed done much to hinder the progress of a modern Christian pilgrim, unless he was already well started on his path. But the layering of Christendom with beliefs, practices, and rituals that have little to do with the simple preaching and practice of Christ Jesus has been the main cause for the decline of Christianity as the vital force it must again become. Without in any way criticizing the steps in Christian history that have themselves been major stepping stones in the Western world's progress, the purpose of this book is to try to show how Christian Scientists believe that the articulation given Christianity by Mary Baker Eddy is the path to spirituality that so many honest men and women are seeking.

In the end, Christianity is about the spiritualization of thought and action. In the end, it is still about being born again, as Jesus told Nicodemus he must be if he was to see the kingdom of God.

Mrs. Eddy wrote in an article called "One Cause and Effect," "As the ages advance in spirituality, Christian Science will be seen to depart from the trend of other Christian denominations in no wise except by increase of spirituality."[18] We are not yet ready to tackle the rather simple metaphysical system that constitutes the theology of Christian Science, but it would be well even at the outset to make clear that Christian Science is not some kind of mind-healing cult or antimedical system whose adherents act in ignorance of the amazing accomplishments of medicine and biotechnology today. It is, rather, a well-articulated exposition of very traditional Christian doctrine that mortal man must indeed be born again, that much of what this world offers must be laid aside, or at least not accepted on its own terms, in order to enjoy the fruits of being a Christian. Its benefits can be immediate, but, being basic Christianity, it requires consistent commitment and practice. It happens, coincidentally (but, Christian Scientists believe, not by accident), to have come at a late enough stage of human civilization that its statement can be understood and practiced by an indefinite number of generations to follow those who are trying to leave some imprint for good in these closing days of the twentieth century.

The language of Christian Science is *sui generis*, a fact that has contributed to the popular impression that Christian Science lies farther from the mainstream of orthodoxy than it actually does. Yet this language is not complicated, but, just like the language of any discipline or profession, requires familiarity on the part of the user. The language may be unique and, as applied to Christianity, new, but the message is old.

"Ye must be born again," Christian Scientists would say, is not only the demand of Christ Jesus, but the inward yearning of every human being who feels intuitively that what the material senses tell him about life and offer him of life is not enough.

Christian Scientists would, in fact, consider themselves born-again Christians if the phrase were used in a slightly altered meaning. Mrs. Eddy did not think that the acquisition of spirituality came easily; she had too much of the John Bunyan approach to Christianity in her to accept the easy conversion route. This is not to say that the decision to turn toward the Christ cannot come quickly or suddenly, although it is more often a kind of inner conviction that grows bit by bit.

We might remember that, in early New England, the conversion experience was not a part of orthodoxy (there will be more about this in chapter 6). But well before the time of Mrs. Eddy, who was a child in the 1820s and 1830s, the idea of a conversion experience had become a part of the Calvinism she knew as a child. She very much rejected this concept but also very much believed that man must be born again. In an essay called "The New Birth," she wrote:

> The new birth is not the work of a moment. It begins with moments, and goes on with years; moments of surrender to God, of childlike trust and joyful adoption of good; moments of self-abnegation, self-consecration, heaven-born hope, and spiritual love. Time may commence, but it cannot complete, the new birth: eternity does this; for progress is the law of infinity.[19]

CHRISTIANS; IN THE WORLD BUT NOT OF IT

Having claimed a born-again heritage for Christian Scientists, this is perhaps also the place to at least address the age-old question that all Christians must answer: are we in this world or out of it? It may help to give some hint of where Christian Science stands even before discussing the details of the religion. It also directly addresses this question of the relegation of religion to a more minor role in life, since standing apart from the world could mean either accepting little responsibility or concern for the problems of our time or taking up those problems from a different standpoint than does the majority of mankind.

Jesus gave us the direction: "My kingdom is not of this world."[20] Yet by all he said and did, he changed events in "this" world. He gave the ultimate ethical instructions, to do unto others as we would have them do unto us. He healed every kind of physical incapacity, leaving people free to carry on more normal, fruitful activities. He performed even mightier feats over what most would consider inviolable material laws—such as multiplying the loaves and fishes, changing water into wine, walking on the water, calming the storm, raising Lazarus from the dead, and eventually overcoming death himself. Yet he saw Judaism (and let us always remember that besides the titles

Christianity has bestowed on Jesus, he was also popularly called "rabbi") as demanding a new ethic and, as Mrs. Eddy would later say, an entirely new look at what constitutes reality in the light of God's omnipotence.

Persecution often forced the early Christians into being "not of this world." They banded together for self-protection. They also mistakenly, for the first hundred years or even longer, expected Jesus' physical return, and this belief would have acted to keep them separate from the aims of the rest of society. However, even considering that early period apart from the rest of Christian history, there was a deeper reason for Christians to have their own agenda. What had caused them to leave their nets, their safety as citizens of the Roman Empire swearing allegiance to Greek or Roman deities, was a new view of reality. They had in very fact experienced the new birth in themselves. Their conception of God's power, as seen through the works of Jesus, became so real to them that they would willingly endure any persecution that might be visited upon them.

Aside from the exigencies of persecution or the expected physical return of Jesus, there were from the beginning some Christians who did not believe in perpetuating the race. This extreme form of chastity has persisted through the ages. Those who have no spiritual inclination at all view this as a form of self-denial that denigrates the value of life itself. However, if one tries to understand what positive value this position might have held either for an individual or for society, he or she can appreciate that it had its source in a living conception of God that made all the normal parts of a so-called earthly life seem impediments to spiritual progress.

Margaret Miles, a professor at the Harvard Divinity School, addressed the issue of asceticism in a baccalaureate speech in 1980. Without trying to restore the negative parts of asceticism, she placed it, including such practices as the renunciation of sex, in its historical and, I think, proper setting.

> Before Christianity was knowledge, before it was rectified moral commitments, even before it was community, Christian faith was explicitly an orientation to the source of life. This hasn't impressed us enough. We tend to fatigue very rapidly in the strength and intensity of this language:

Irenaeus: True life comes from partaking in God ...

Origen: He takes away the deadness in us ...

Augustine: ... only they can think of God without absurdity who think of him as life itself.

Miles says that one early Eucharistic prayer went: "We beg you, make us truly alive." She continues:

> Now, this sense of being "truly alive"—of finally getting straight about where life comes from—seemed, to these early Christians, to contain an implicit critique of secular culture. They saw secular culture as locating the essential concerns of the human being in the pursuit of sex, power, and possessions. . . . they were prepared to back with their lives this rejection of the secular analysis of human life.[21]

Asceticism, she says, aimed to be about more life—it was a tool "for locating and eliminating deadness." That it went awry in hair-shirt practices, or even, many would say, in the much more common acts of celibacy or fasting, should not cloud its origins. Men have wanted, for twenty centuries, to follow the Master's way; but the instruction did not seem complete. Hence the manifold avenues Christianity has taken.

To come up to today, fewer Christians are thinking of becoming celibate. In fact, there is even a movement among some Roman Catholic clergy to allow married clergy in their church once again. Nor, given the widespread need in Western culture for a higher demonstration of morality, honesty, and mutual consideration in marital relations, does celibacy seem to most people like a reasonable or realistic goal on the agenda for social morality. However, this is only one of the more extreme examples of the many situations Christians have faced over the years in trying to follow Christ Jesus, and is probably more illustrative than any other example of the degree to which sincere Christians have been willing to leave the patterns of this world if they felt such a departure would help them become better followers of Christ.

The theologian Richard Niebuhr looked on this issue of a Christian's standing apart from the world in terms of Christ versus culture. He identified at least five different approaches, which are given in abbreviated form in a book written by William Fore, a United Methodist minister who worked at the National Council of Churches in New York for over two decades and is now teaching at Yale. They are, in skeletal form:

1. Christ against culture.
2. Christ of culture.
3. Christ above culture.
4. Christ and culture in paradox.
5. Christ the transformer of culture.[22]

The Christ against culture syndrome is best characterized by some of the fundamentalist approaches to worldly entertainment—shunning the theater, movies, dancing, all those activities that supposedly lead to personal immorality. This approach, strangely, does not usually include as strong a critique of the shortcomings of American democracy or of our system of business. Christ versus culture would require a wholesale rejection of many aspects of life today, if it were to be as critical of other areas as it is of so-called worldly entertainment. Moreover, the Christ versus culture approach most typically is popular among uneducated people who have little appreciation for the bonding, or civilizing, influence that comes from artistic achievements that can be shared by all, or for the ways in which great truths and moral issues are often given new insight by their treatment in one of the art forms.

The Christ of culture, according to Rev. Fore, is the way of liberal, cultural Protestantism. It is akin to the social gospel preached at the end of the last century, which portrayed Jesus as a liberal social reformer. To the degree that society has advanced because of the ideal of human equality before God laid out by Jesus, the Christian cannot feel a total rejection of his society. But the all-too-easy identification of social liberalism with Christianity may be one reason the mainline, more liberal Protestant churches have been losing membership relative to the more conservative evangelical churches in the last twenty years. Those looking for a more spiritual life would seem to feel that, even if liberty, social justice, and an end to inequities bred into the law are worthy goals, they are a long way off from defining the totality of Christianity.

The other three approaches have something in common with one another, and it is in this general area that one would place Christian Science. The ideal held up by Christ Jesus is always above what human society has achieved, but it is in that society that the ideal must be worked out. Christian perfection is the goal of the Christian Scientist. One may grow spiritually while he or she is living an isolated life; in fact, modern life almost requires of us some individual moments in the desert or on the mountaintop. But many of the moral qualities—for instance, honesty, compassion, justice—have meaning only in relation to other people, and our possession of these qualities is tested and demonstrated through contact with others. This is the only way, in fact, in which one's Christianity comes to have a positive impact on all the elements of a culture.

If there is a temptation for Christians in the rich West to accept the all-too-easy life that many of them have (in material terms), this temptation is equally present for Christian Scientists. As we shall see, one purpose of the major publishing activities carried on by the Christian Science Publishing Society is to maintain the productive tension that must always exist between those who have a spiritual ideal and the society in which they are trying to implement it. In his last message to his disciples, Jesus said: "In the world ye shall have tribulation: but be of good cheer; I have overcome the world."[23]

There will be a short discussion of the life of Mary Baker Eddy in chapter 6. It should be mentioned here, however, that in her own life experience she was very nearly the kind of ascetic described by Margaret Miles—having little use for the pleasures of the flesh (including the table!), withdrawing many times a day for lengthy prayer and meditation, taking no rest from what she saw as her religious mission in a forty-five-year period that stretched from her forty-fifth year into her ninetieth. Yet the entire purpose of the mission she saw for Christian Science was to establish a kind of practice of

Christianity that would eventually reach into the entire world and revolutionize the world's thinking about theology, health, and the structure of reality. In fact, those who are most assiduously practicing Christian Science would say that their religion is changing their thought about what kind of world they actually do live in! But in terms of more traditional Christian expression, let us leave this chapter with the statement that Christian Scientists strive to be in the world, but not of it.

Chapter 3

THE PHYSICAL SCIENCES TODAY

There is a widespread assumption that the advances of the physical sciences and the technologies spawned by scientific knowledge have diminished the sphere of religion. This assumption found one articulate echo in some of the material on secularization quoted in the previous chapter.

Popular assumptions frequently fall wide of the mark, however, in this era of instant communications. Habits of thought are still formed over a period of years, if not decades, and the bases on which edifices of a mass philosophy or approach to living are erected may have crumbled by the time the edifice is completed. Such is actually the case with the physical sciences in terms of their relationship with revealed religions. The perception that science and religion are opposed may be more a nineteenth-century stereotype than a twentieth, particularly if one considers William James's discussion of the continuing need men and women have to see the universe from the center of their own individual existence in it. Moreover, many of those scientists who stand on the cutting edge of theory survey the complexity of the physical universe and conclude that there must be a unifying force and even a purpose behind it.

MODERN MAN WITHOUT A HOME

The twentieth century has witnessed the breakdown of the Newtonian view of the universe. Before the time of Newton, Western philosophies that dealt with world cosmology had hummed some version of the classical tune composed by Aristotle. In the thirteenth century, Aristotle had been updated, as it were, by Thomas Aquinas. Aquinas did his work against the backdrop of new (to European eyes) scientific knowledge that became available after Christian victories on the battlefield against the Moslem Moors living in Spain.

Changes in worldview take place infrequently. Those that have occurred in the Western world can be counted on the fingers of one hand: that of Aristotle, the melding of worldly philosophy and Christian theology under Augustine in the first decades of the fifth century, the work of Thomas Aquinas in the thirteenth, and then the Newtonian revolution. Newton published his *Principia Mathematica* in 1687, and the era beginning then and continuing until the time of Einstein became dominated by a mechanistic view of nature and even of man. This mechanistic view encouraged empirical observation and experimentation even more than was the case at the time of the Renaissance. (It also encouraged a mechanistic view of man and the medical arts, treating man's body as something separate from his mentality. This overemphasis has continued until recent times, when even in the medical field there has been the beginning of a more holistic approach to healing.) The world of cause and effect, of physical laws that allowed for a God only as a first cause or overall superintendent of the universe, certainly contributed heavily to the decline of the grip that revealed religious dogma had had on men's minds.

In the world of ordinary affairs, much of the Newtonian view still holds. However, beginning with several discoveries in both the micro world of atoms, electrons, and protons and in the macro world of light waves passing through eons of time in a universe that may be ten or fifteen billion years old, Newtonian physics does not hold. Physicists have discovered different orders of reality. Many of their discoveries lie behind the common modern inventions we all use. The light from your television screen is the emission of electrons that cannot be seen even by the finest instruments (although their position can be shown by means of photography, thus verifying their existence).

But what is an atom? Almost entirely empty space. The writers of one book, trying to explain the near impossibility of envisioning an atom, describe the proportions of the simple hydrogen atom (one electron and one proton) as the proton being the size of a marble, with the electron the size of a thirty-foot-diameter balloon in motion around the marble at a distance of half a mile. The rate of motion? It makes 100,000,000,000,000 revolutions a second![1]

Another phenomenon of which the human mind cannot really have a mental picture is the nature of light rays. Light exhibits the characteristics of both a wave in motion and a particle. But how can something be both a wave and a particle? Common sense tells us it cannot be both. Yet that is the way physicists have come to think about light. And it is that mental construct of light that has yielded the best empirical results. So, is that the truth about light, or is it merely the most that can be said about it at this stage of our understanding?

The more we have learned about the nature of the physical universe, the more difficult it has become to envision the place of man in that universe. We are cosmologies away from the comforting but erroneous view that heaven really was in the heavens and that the angels were intermediaries traveling back and forth between the two spheres. But is the only alternative the bleak view of Bertrand Russell, who saw man at the end of the trail of animal evolution, living in a universe that would gradually grow dim and itself die?

The Jewish philosopher Martin Buber, who spent most of his later years as a professor in Palestine (before the creation of the State of Israel), wrote about this question of man's lack of a spiritual home in the twentieth century and his quest for one. He addressed the issue in a rather difficult essay, "What Is Man?"

He went through an intellectual romp of the periods in which man has had a home and those in which he has, so to speak, had to live in a makeshift tent. The essay is apropos today, for he finds man essentially homeless in today's world.

> In the history of the human spirit, I distinguish between epochs of habitation and epochs of homelessness. In the former, man lives in the world as in a house, as in a home. In the latter, man lives in the world as in an open field and at times does not even have four pegs with which to set up a tent.[2]

There have been three great attempts in Western thought to build a home for man, Buber says—three attempts to settle once and for all man's place in the universe, to give him the comfort of a home that in his spiritual depths he yearns for. The first was the world cosmogony built by Aristotle before the time of Christ; the second was the medieval Catholic world, which rose to its heights in the philosophy of Thomas Aquinas; the third was the more modest attempt of Hegel to set up a dialectic.

"Aristotle's cosmological image of the universe breaks up from within, through the soul's experience of the problem of evil in its depth, and through its feeling of being surrounded by a divided universe," Buber writes; "Aquinas's theological image of the universe breaks up from without, through the universe manifesting itself as unlimited."[3] Hegel's contribution in this area was his belief in the purposes of an Absolute—God? Each age, according to Hegel, fulfilled its destiny in working on a structure whose completion it could not, from its own limited viewpoint, hope to understand. Hegel wrote at the end of the period of grandiose philosophical superstructures. Unfortunately, he is most popularly remembered today for the capture and misappropriation of his idea of the historic dialectic (this inexorable process of history to which each age contributes) by Karl Marx.

There is a small difference from the cosmologies I identified at the start of the chapter, in that Buber does not mention Augustine and substitutes Hegel for Newton. But in the first instance we are discussing the Christian synthesis, first with Plato and later with Aristotle, that dominated the Dark Ages and the Middle Ages in both theology and physics, and in the second instance we are talking about the Western revolt from medievalism. Newton represented the revolt in physics; Hegel, the last major attempt to adjust to a new order in philosophy.

My purpose in referring to Aristotle, Aquinas, or even Hegel in this space is to reach Martin Buber's main thesis: Today's cosmology does not give a picture of the universe that seems to satisfy what one would generally call man's "inner needs." The physical sciences have, for most of us, removed the comfort of home.

> Einstein's concept of the universe signifies no fulfillment of the spirit's inkling, but the contradiction of all its inklings and imaginings; this universe can still be thought, but it can no longer be imaged, the man who thinks it no longer really lives in it. The generation which works modern cosmology into its natural thought will be the first, after several millennia of changing images of the universe, which will have to forego the possession of an image of its universe; this very fact, that it lives in a universe which cannot be imaged, will probably be its feeling of the universe, so to speak its image of the universe.[4]

ROOM FOR MULTIPLE REALITIES?

What Buber is saying, it seems to me, is that the universe we have come to know in modern physics provides no mental comfort or spiritual resting place within its own framework. But this is not to say that man does not have a home anywhere. One of the ways to approach this question is to acknowledge that the process by which scientific discovery takes place in the physical universe is not the only kind of mental activity of which man is capable. What is needed for the perception of one aspect or realm of experience may be entirely different from what is needed for another; some of the farthest advanced theoretical physicists have themselves dared to talk about multiple realms of reality.

Now, any discussion of multiple kinds of reality may seem as difficult to envision as an electron orbiting its proton or the path of light wave/particles. Yet the description of the atom and the description of the light wave/particle have produced multiple new sciences, and one's inability to have a picture of them in his mind does not mean that that particular mental construct is inaccurate as far as it goes.

Something of what this is leading up to was foreseen by Immanuel Kant, the late eighteenth-century German philosopher who is almost as hard to understand as are the modern physicists. Kant began his life as a scientist, although in those days the spheres of the philosopher and the scientist were still not entirely separate. (Nor, as we shall see, are they today.) Even in his scientific writings he was striving to reconcile the state of eighteenth-century scientific knowledge with religion. His own family background was Pietist, a central European sect that stressed a more direct "experience" with God than did the larger Evangelical church of Luther's.

Our interest in Kant here is that, as he switched his interest from the natural sciences to philosophy, his field became the study of epistemology—how do we know what we think we know? And, without going into the details of the difficult treatises he wrote in the 1770s and 1780s, we can pull out of them one of his dominant themes: that the construction of the human mind goes a long way toward determining our perceptions. Space, time, and even causation are fixed concepts in the human mind, he argued. They are what philosophic language calls "a priori constructions"; that is, they exist independently of and prior to the senses' experience of them. And it is their existence that gives coherence to what the senses perceive.

This particular approach did not survive the centuries intact, but it did open up a major new avenue of exploration for philosophy and later for the developing field of psychology. The construction of the human mind, in other words, is itself a factor in how physical reality is perceived. Whether time and space are solely constructs, or ideas, of this mind is debatable. But here is a philosopher, roughly four generations before the time of Einstein, struggling with new definitions of time and space. (In the Einsteinian world of relativity, they meant something quite different from what they meant for Kant, of course.)

With Kant, the entirely objective physical world of Newton begins to break down. There is the beginning of an understanding that we human beings are not passive observers of the creation but that at least some part of human thought itself plays a role in fashioning the outside world. As Buber writes:

> . . . there is in the world a being who knows the universe as a universe, its space as space, its time as time, and knows himself in it as knowing it. . . . If a being has emerged from the animal world who knows about life and about his own life, then the fact and the manner of this emergence cannot be explained by his place in the animal world or comprehended by concepts of nature.[5]

To advance quickly from the end of the eighteenth century to the end of the nineteenth, let us look once again at the Edinburgh lectures of William James. After devoting two of his lectures to the transformation experiences of Christians of his day (in the main, the examples were British), James said that the "claims of the sectarian scientists are, to say the least, premature." While the experiences he related had more to do with a new vision of life (the kind of revitalization that Margaret Miles spoke of in her sermon on asceticism, and not with physical healing as such), he also touched on the phenomenon of physical healing resulting from a change of thought.

James resurrected an idea that sounds very similar to Kant's categories of the mind. The experiences of religiously oriented people, he said, show

> the universe to be a more many-sided affair than any sect, even the scientific sect, allows for. What, in the end, are all our verifications but experiences that agree with more or less isolated systems of ideas (conceptual systems) that our minds have framed? *But why in the name of common sense need we assume that only one such system of ideas can be true?* [The world can be] handled according to many systems of ideas, and is so handled by different men, and will each time give some characteristic kind of profit, for which he cares, to the handler, while at the same time some other kind of profit has to be omitted or postponed. . . . [Science and religion can both be] genuine keys for unlocking the world's treasure-house. . . . Just as evidently neither is exhaustive or exclusive of the other's simultaneous use. And why, after all, may not the world *be so complex as to consist of many interpenetrating spheres of reality?*[6]

Today it is not as uncommon as it was one hundred years ago to talk about different types of reality. Yet that concept seems to defy common sense, which still yearns for a unified explanation of every phenomenon in our lives and in the universe. Lawrence Leshan, a New York psychologist, and Henry Margenau, Yale professor of physics emeritus, write in a book called *Einstein's Space and Van Gogh's Sky:*

> Perhaps one reason why it is so difficult for us to accept the idea of multiple, equally valid realities is that so much that made the world stable and permanent, Gibraltarlike and reassuring, has already been taken away from us. The earth was unique, and the center of the universe until the work of Kepler and Copernicus told us otherwise. Man was descended from God and made in His image until Darwin told us otherwise. Our reason was an absolute tool with which we could understand the world and logically react until Freud told us otherwise. Our customs and social beliefs reflected eternal verities and told us what was absolutely right and was absolutely wrong until the modern anthropologists told us otherwise. What was left was the idea of truth: that there was one truth and that, at least, was unique, stable, and eternal. . . . And now science seems to be taking this last bastion of stability in a frightening universe away from us. Is it a wonder that we resist?[7]

Before we resist the concept of multiple realities too strongly, however, we should remind ourselves that we are talking about definitions created by the human mind. We are talking about multiple realities only in the sense that that is how the human mind is presently able to comprehend the individual's experience in the world. It is perhaps the ultimate ego trip to think that the human mind, itself a product of biological evolution and as ephemeral as the rest of human life, can be the ultimate possessor of truth. Perhaps it is enough for now if, instead of accepting the difficult concept of multiple realities, one can at least say, "Ah, yes, I can understand that there are many ways of *approaching* reality. Perhaps for occasion X this way works best and for occasion Y another approach is more effective."

The discoveries of twentieth-century science have actually opened a door toward the possibility of a spiritual explanation of reality that seemed to have been lost by Newtonian physics. Many of the discoveries in the physical sciences have not been of a nature to explain all physical phenomena as much as they have been answers to particular sets of problems physicists were working with. If physicists have themselves backed off somewhat from the search for a single theory of all physical phenomena (and remember that few of them gave much intellectual support to Einstein's search for a unified field theory), perhaps we can see more easily that there is also room for a series of spiritual phenomena—even if these phenomena resist explanation by the same mind-set that perceives the world of physics.

Leshan and Margenau say:

> Science today, both in physics and in the social sciences, has brought us to the point where we must face the fact that if we wish to proceed on the scientific path and attempt to make our data lawful, we simply cannot have only one set of principles about how reality works. We need to allow for a number of alternate realities.[8]

While the commonsense mind rejects the concept of multiple realities, there is this much to say for it: Newtonian physics, within its sphere, works. The micro and macro discoveries of the twentieth century, which show Newton to have been incorrect in some areas, work—work in the sense of producing practical new technologies.

Now, the experience of mankind also tells us that we have an inner spiritual life that exists independently of the brain. It may express itself verbally at times, but what most of mankind means by spirit has to do with a sense that is expressed through every organ of the body in some way that suggests tranquillity, inner harmony, wholeness, oneness with mankind and the universe, peace, dispassionate love, timelessness, and so on. And many would say that they are conscious of the spiritual in a way that has nothing to do with body at all. Because the spiritual deals with the inner life, it is not as easily measurable, if indeed it can be measured at all. Because it is experienced subjectively, it cannot be recognized objectively—although its results, as in a changed bodily or mental condition, are objectified.

The experience of mankind since the time of Newton has been to see the role of the spiritual gradually narrowed. While not all physicists today would agree with one another, there is a sense of great humility among many of them about the meaning of what they are finding. That, along with this concept of multiple realities, at least gives mankind a way to talk about one facet of experience that most people feel is a part of them. In fact, the day may be at hand when the fragmented nature of today's theoretical physics makes allowance for a category that we intuit as the spiritual.

In a television series produced for the British Broadcasting Corporation by James Burke early in the 1980s, called "The Day the Universe Changed," Burke traced the major scientific advances since the end of the Middle Ages. Sounding very much like the Immanuel Kant of two centuries ago, Burke said in his concluding segment:

> Reality, in one sense, is in the brain before it is experienced, or else the signals would make no sense. The brain imposes visual order on chaos by grouping sets of signals, rearranging them, or rejecting them. Reality is what the brain makes it. . . . This imposition of the hypothesis . . . modifies all forms of perception at all levels of complexity. To quote Wittgenstein [the Viennese-born philosopher who taught at Cambridge in the first half of this century], "You see what you want to see." . . . All observation of the external world is, therefore, theory-laden. The world would be chaos if this were not so.[9]

If we can concede even partially that we cannot see what we are not prepared to see, it should be obvious that the gradual elimination of spiritual phenomena from the realm of respectable scientific discussion has had a role in diminishing man's consciousness of the spiritual world. In the present position of the advanced theoretical sciences one sees at least a glimmer that in this age "the earth will help the woman." That reference, for those who do not know the Bible well, is to the twelfth chapter of the Book of Revelation, in which John sees the reign of the kingdom of God coming to earth in spite of attempts to postpone its appearing. Mrs. Eddy likened the woman in this case to the appearing of the perfect, spiritual manhood of each individual child of God—and, because the time was ripe for the appearing (human thought was prepared for it), the earth assisted its appearance.

Because mankind at least partly sees what it is prepared to see, giving admittance to the reality of spirituality could open up major new vistas of experience. We understand in retrospect how the Newtonian view of the universe tended to make much of human experience fall into line with what men thought Newton was saying. God as the watchmaker might still rule, but God in his aspects as a loving Father or a comforting Mother seemed too anthropomorphic for the intellectuals of the eighteenth and nineteenth centuries. If God, or the role of spirituality in human experience, was again a more widely shared view, we would begin to see more evidence of the validity of spirituality in general. One can recognize and admit that the subjective nature of one's experience of spirituality is such that it cannot be broached in the same manner that one talks about superconductivity experiments. Nor will a scientific age admit a spirituality that, in spite of its subjective nature, cannot be commonly "handled" by all. In other words, it cannot be a complete mystery and gain access to thinking people today. But more of us first need to admit its possibility if we hope to experience any of its fruits.

MRS. EDDY AND THE PHYSICAL SCIENCES; DARWIN AND FREUD

Since the chapter on the metaphysical system of Christian Science deals largely with traditional biblical terminology or theological concepts, this may be the best place to introduce a short explanation of the place Mrs. Eddy saw for the physical sciences in relation to Christian Science. In a word, she did to the physical sciences what their theoreticians had done to the world of religion for three hundred years. She pushed the border back. Having based her metaphysical system on the allness of a spiritual God, she found no place within that system for a material universe. But rather than calling the physical universe a mistake (as some of the gnostics did), she said that it was a mistaken, or limited, sense of existence entertained in the human mind.

Actually, she did not in any disciplined sense try to interweave her metaphysical system with the physical sciences. She was not a student of modern science, to begin with, although she welcomed the overcoming of human limitations that the sciences made possible. The universe she had come to know, through her study of the Bible, was a spiritual universe. This universe became as tangible to her as the physical realities that were being measured by the increasingly sophisticated instruments of natural scientists in their laboratories. The natural world of astronomy, physics, chemistry, biology, and anthropology existed—from the standpoint of spiritual thinking—as a kind of misstatement, or at best a partial and limited view of the reality apparent to spiritual sense. She wrote: "The myriad forms of mortal thought, made manifest as matter, are not more distinct nor real to the material senses than are the Soul-created forms to spiritual sense, which cognizes Life as permanent" (Soul and Life being used by her as synonymous with God).[10]

But like the natural scientist—and this is why she felt she could attach the name Science to Christianity—she demanded proof of her position. This was what Christian Science healing provided. The metaphysics of Christian Science, she claimed, gave man the basis he needed for living—for right relationships with others, for healing his physical and mental illnesses, for purpose in life, and the assurance of the continuity of consciousness.

In effect, a spiritually scientific system of metaphysics could overrule the process of so-called natural law in the thought and experience of the person who was sufficiently aware of spiritual laws. The process at work in society at large, by which the tree of Christianity was being denuded of its branches of authority one by one, has been reversed by Christian Science. The person whose thought is dwelling in scientific metaphysics can come to experience a constant sense of God's presence, power, and loving control that has greater reality to him than whatever physics, biology, or the doctrine of human evolution may tell him about man. In terms of the discussion of the past few pages, Mrs. Eddy laid claim to a spiritual reality with which modern, scientific thought would eventually have to grapple.

It is not going beyond the limits of historical credibility to say that a system denominated Christian Science and expressing itself in lan-

guage somewhat similar to Mrs. Eddy's could not have been founded
before human thinking had generally moved to a rational or scientific plane. The thoughts to which Christian Science turns men and
women were not discovered through the processes of human reason.
But it certainly became much easier for large numbers of people to
consider God in the terms Mrs. Eddy uses when civilization as a
whole had come to considering the universe, for instance, in terms
of cause and effect, not in terms that allowed a role for a deity or
deities of capriciousness, whimsy, or arbitrariness.

One other factor about the timeliness of the discovery of Christian
Science is its connection, or lack of connection, with either the evo-
lutionary terminology of Darwin or the psychological jargon of Freud
and his successors. Since Mrs. Eddy says very little about Darwin and
appears to have known nothing of Freud, one may ask whether her
language would have been different had she been writing twenty or
fifty years later. Perhaps, but probably not in any major way. Her
description of man metaphysically would not have changed, any more
than her descriptive terms for God. Her vision of a totally spiritual
universe protected her metaphysical system from invasion by any concepts dealing with matter's reality.

Her references to the human situation, however, would almost
surely have been somewhat different. Since Darwin and Freud were
the two big names dominating twentieth-century anthropological
thought, one might wish today that Mrs. Eddy could have dealt with
them. One way to look at this is to consider that perhaps Christian
Science actually does deal with them, at least by indirection.

Mrs. Eddy was aware of Darwin's theory of evolution in general.
She said in one of the earlier editions of *Science and Health* that
Darwin was right in his theory of evolution. Then, out of her intuition that even the most unchallenged scientific theory can someday
be challenged, she said more circumspectly, "In its history of mortality, Darwin's theory of evolution from a material basis is more consistent than most theories."[11] Since she at no point saw mortal,
material man as developing into the individual representation of the
Christ, which is man's only actual selfhood, she was not interested
in mortal history per se. In fact, in the flyleaf to her *Miscellaneous
Writings*, she included a short poem she had written:

If worlds were formed by matter,
  and mankind from the dust;
Till time shall end more timely,
  There's nothing here to trust.
Thenceforth to evolution's
  Geology, we say,—
Nothing have we gained therefrom,
  And nothing have to pray:
My world has sprung from Spirit,
  In everlasting day;
Whereof, I've more to glory,
  Wherefore, have much to pay.[12]

It did not matter to her, as it did to the fundamentalists of her own generation or ours, whether the universe was six thousand years old (as William Jennings Bryan maintained in the Scopes "monkey trial" in 1925) or six billion years old. This was not "her" universe. Geologists, anthropologists, and other experts in the physical and biological sciences would continue to conceptualize patterns of development in their respective fields, while her metaphysical system would show how to correct and overcome the human limitations inherent in those very conceptions of reality.

To some who try to make a purely intellectual leap from the material to the spiritual, it seems incongruous that a perfect spiritual man, expressing all the faculties and qualities one can attribute to divinity, could exist while a material man was slowly coming into being through the blind processes of evolution. The difficulty may be at least partly resolved by understanding that, although the material can be described as a false concept of the spiritual and real, there is no actual counterpart relationship. Christian Science does not present a system of metaphysical dualism, in which matter is either the reflection or the shadow of Spirit. But it is necessary to include within the metaphysical language of Christian Science "due notice" to the fact that mankind in general thinks differently.

As for Freud, it is probably true that more young Americans today are familiar with Freudian terminology than with the concepts of Christianity, orthodox or otherwise. Repression, frustration, transference, the Oedipus complex, the basic categories of the id, ego, and superego, are in general use, as is the language of many of the branches of analysis that have sprung from the Freudian tree of knowledge. The level of popular understanding about many of these terms, unfortunately, may strike the Freudians as being as muddled as is the popular understanding of religious and metaphysical terms.

Two of the major contributions Freud made to people's thinking about themselves were the role of the unconscious and the strength of the sex drive. But Freud was not the first to be aware of the unconscious. Mrs. Eddy herself frequently mentions the unconscious thoughts of mortals. Sometimes she connects this phrase with the brain, or matter in general, since her system recognizes no sharp break in the matter-mind continuum. (Both are part of the false concept of creation.) She also sometimes means the thoughts that are hidden in the back of the mind but don't rush forth and say, "Here we are." These are the thoughts that are often the cause of disease, as she explains it.

As for sex, Freud's overemphasis on this already has been partially recognized by other psychologists. And, although it was not part of her "assignment" as she saw it to write in detail about the purely human (and her own taste and background would have acted to prevent it in any case), she was fully aware of what the claims of sex and of human, bodily need in general had to do with holding back the individual's growth toward spiritual reality. She relegated all such concerns to false thinking, which the individual was free to resist anytime he wanted to. Whether Mrs. Eddy fully appreciated what most people today rather blithely accept as the biological claims regarding sexual urgency, her spiritual vision (and therefore the direction in which she tried to lead thought) would have been unaltered. She wrote, for instance, "That body is most harmonious in which the discharge of the natural functions is least noticeable."[13] Christianity, as she saw the life of Jesus, had not come to give comfort to those who wished to prolong the dream of material living.

✳ ✳ ✳

Mrs. Eddy saw Christian Science as science, but always foremost as a return to primitive Christianity. There is, however, as this brief discussion of changing ways of looking at the universe has shown, never a way to go back to the past in the sense of repeating it. We still find our spiritual home in Christianity, but as Thomas Wolfe found when he wrote about his North Carolina boyhood of the early twentieth century, "You Can't Go Home Again." One does not live with the identical cosmological view today; neither are the social or political conditions similar. The sense in which Mrs. Eddy meant to restore primitive Christianity was to reach back to the simple Bible record, the most authoritative source available as to what Jesus really taught and did, and to restore as a normal practice among humankind his method of healing as well as his ethical and moral imperatives. She saw Jesus' life as establishing the pattern by which Christians should live as long as there is a human race. "The purpose of his great life-work extends through time and includes universal humanity."[14]

Virtually every reform and new religious order within the Roman Catholic church has had to some degree the same intent, of going back to the beginning and rediscovering the freshness of life that the new birth of Christianity brings to human beings. This has also been the stated aim of the various branches of Protestantism. Christian Scientists would say, however, that no one has so broken through the incrustation of the centuries to find the key to Jesus' life as did Mary Baker Eddy. And the proof they would offer of that claim is the relatively successful record of healing that they have laid down for over one hundred years—healing in a broad sense, but also in the specific sense of replicating much of the record Jesus left.

In his television series, James Burke rather dramatically portrayed modern science as beginning on the day that the Spanish, with the aid of French nobles, broke through to Toledo, captured its library, and expelled the Moslems. Amazed at the high level of Moorish Arab learning, they rediscovered Aristotle and the Greek rational mind. To this were added the Arabs' own scientific advances of the first millennium. While Greece itself was not restored in the process, the rediscovery of Greece was the beginning of the end of the Middle Ages, the beginning of the rise of modern science and rationalism.

We cannot return to the first century or the first millennium. But it is just as possible that there was a level of spiritual consciousness activated by Jesus and present for several generations that will ultimately have as much meaning for mankind as the Greek logical mind has had for modern times.

Adolf von Harnack, a German biblical scholar, speaking at the end of the nineteenth century, said:

> The great English philosopher, John Stuart Mill, has somewhere observed that mankind cannot be too often reminded that there was once a man of the name of Socrates. That is true; but still more important is it to remind mankind again and again that a man of the name of Jesus Christ once stood in their midst.[15]

A rediscovery of the meaning of Jesus' life and works can do for mankind in the late twentieth century what the rediscovery of the Greeks did for European civilization at the end of the Middle Ages; and to many of her followers, Mrs. Eddy's discovery of Christian Science can be of broad relevance to humanity in the general Christian rediscovery.

Before getting to that discovery, however, there is still more background to lay out. Let us look in the next chapter at the nature of early Christianity, particularly at the debates its theologians had over issues that have come to a new resolution in the presentation of Christian Science.

Chapter 4

THE EARLY CHURCH

The preceding chapter indicated the degree to which modern man may often feel homeless in the kind of universe the physicists are describing to him. But, as some of the theoretical physicists have come to see, there are more ways than one of looking at the universe. It still is possible to find home, purpose in life, comfort, and individual peace, even if one is well educated and fully aware of the awesomeness and impersonality of the universe as the physicists describe it. In fact, for the educated Westerner today, nothing may be more important to his or her well-being than learning to view the universe from more than one dimension. Looking at the universe spiritually, learning what the meaning of spirituality is, is not an outdated concept. The prayerful practice of Christianity today fully restores a person's sense of home. It brings a mental and spiritual calm akin to what someone living in a northern climate feels upon arriving home late on a rainy November night, seeing lights in the window, and knowing there is a warm fire in the fireplace and a fresh pot of hot chocolate on the stove.

At this point, we need to look for a moment at the beginnings of Christianity, at the amazing growth the religion experienced in the first few generations after the time of Christ Jesus. For here indeed was a faith that clearly satisfied the spiritual needs of a large cross section of the population in the early centuries of our era.

CONTENT OF THE CHRISTIAN LIFE
MORE IMPORTANT THAN ITS FORM

Most practicing Christians have little knowledge of the practices of early Christians or of the doctrinal debates that emerged as later generations tried to come to grips with the lasting meaning of Christianity for mankind. It is an era that even the academicians cannot re-create as well as they might wish. Many of the early writings have been destroyed, and the dates of events are not always as clear as modern historians would like.

Most scholars agree that no permanent record of Jesus' life was preserved in Hebrew. The Gospels were first written in Greek, and then translated into Latin. The gospel was first explained to the Jews, then to the Gentiles close at hand, then to the Greek-influenced world of the Middle East. Each group of potential converts represented a different mind-set, so one needs to know something about who was being addressed in a particular gospel or letter to know what possible resistance to Christianity was being addressed. The eventual translation into Latin paved the way for Christianity to spread wherever the Roman legions had already gone. Paul and Peter's trips to Rome also foreshadowed the Western route the religion would eventually take. In the early centuries, Antioch (in present-day southern Turkey) and Alexandria were centers rivaling Rome in importance. The spread of Islam throughout the Middle East in the seventh century had much to do with establishing the eventual primacy of Rome in the Western church.

What is clear is that from the small band of apostles and lesser followers of Jesus, a vital religious movement was quickly established. At the start this movement had a minimum of form, but it must have been strong on content—that is, it must have had an inner vigor—to have grown as quickly as it did. The forms and the doctrines came in due time. But let us look first at what is known of the content.

It is nearly impossible from the distance of two thousand years to comprehend how Christianity grew from a tiny band of disciples after the Resurrection to from five to seven million persons who at least claimed the name of Christ by about the year A.D. 300. (By that time it is estimated that the population within the boundaries of the Roman Empire was about 100 million.) There was, as always, more than one reason, but the prime one must have been that Christianity supplied that need for a spiritual home that we human beings have in every age. We know very little about what was preached in the gatherings of Christians in the first hundred years. Henry Chadwick, a British scholar of the early Church, says that the form of service of the early Christians was similar to that of the Jewish synagogues from which they had come—the singing of psalms, reading from the Old Testament, some exegesis on Scripture, and prayers.

In fact, the Christian message was presented first of all to the Jews. At the time of Christ Jesus it has been estimated that of a total population in the Roman Empire of fifty million, some seven million, or 14 percent, were Jewish. It is not generally recognized to what extent the Jews' dispersion throughout the Mediterranean and Middle Eastern world laid the basis for the spread of Christianity. These points are emphasized by the British historian of early Church history, W. H. C. Frend, in his book *The Rise of Christianity*, where he also adds: "By the time of Christ, Judaism was the single most vital religious movement in the Greco-Roman world."[1] Understanding the size and vitality of Jewish communities throughout the area of the Roman Empire may give one a new appreciation for the well-known fact that Christianity was preached first to the Jews.

Presumably these early Christians quickly became acquainted with the Gospels and with the letters of Paul. (The letters of Paul actually came first, beginning in about A.D. 50. Mark, the earliest of the four canonical Gospels, is generally dated at about A.D. 70.) Many other documents also circulated, and it is generally agreed that after the generation of the Apostles the spiritual inspiration in much of the new writing was less vigorous.

One of the early heresies in the fledgling Church had to do with the role of continuing revelation. That was resolved by the decision that the Book of Revelation would be considered the last of the inspired writings, and that with it the age of revelation had come to an end.

Christianity presented a new and satisfying way of life, especially when compared with some of the existing pagan philosophies.

Viewing the early growth of the Church from the standpoint of an eighteenth-century skeptic, Gibbon notes:

> . . . as many were almost disengaged from their artificial prej-
> udices, but equally susceptible and desirous of a devout attach-
> ment, an object much less deserving would have been sufficient
> to fill the vacant place in their hearts, and to gratify the uncer-
> tain eagerness of their passions. Those who are inclined to pur-
> sue this reflection, instead of viewing with astonishment the
> rapid progress of Christianity, will perhaps be surprised that its
> success was not still more rapid and still more universal.[2]

What was the need that Christianity filled? One can summarize it in two ways. First, it presented an ethical system that the world had not yet tested, a system based on love for one's fellowman. This included a strong sense of family and of fidelity within the marriage covenant. This latter element had been a hallmark of Judaism as well, but Christianity had the advantage of being presented to the world as a universal religion. Second, it proposed that man is much more than a sinning mortal; it demonstrated a higher vision of man in continuing for some time to repeat the works of Jesus and in promising its adherents eternal life.

What both the pagans of Rome and the skeptics of the Enlightenment in Europe all seemed to agree on is that the early Christians did practice what was then and would still today be considered an amazing degree of brotherly love. "The contempt of the world exercised them in the habits of humility, meekness, and patience. The more they were persecuted, the more closely they adhered to each other. Their mutual charity and unsuspecting confidence has been remarked by infidels, and was too often abused by perfidious friends."[3] This sense of practical charity is probably the element that most accounts for their cohesion and growth in the first two or three centuries.

The new religion also cut across class lines, even though it did not offer (nor would it have been able to deliver) political emancipation to women or slaves. "It was consciously aimed at the common people, and the ideals of simplicity and humility were never far from the minds of those who had to propagate their faith. . . . in a world that was acutely conscious of rank and class . . . the Christians deliberately set out to treat the poor with dignity and without condescension."[4]

Wherever they gathered, they repeated their Lord's Last Supper. Theology was not yet developed enough for disagreements over the nature of the sacraments; the simple meal demonstrated their consecration to the ideal of Jesus' life. Chadwick notes the deep human need that the simple early Christian ritual filled. ". . . baptism and admission to the sacred meal meant a break with the past and a gift of grace by which the individual could live up to ideals and moral imperatives recognized by his conscience. In a word, Christianity directly answered to the human quest for true happiness—by which more is meant than feeling happy!"[5]

As for the healing works of the early Church, even skeptical writers also seem to agree that for several generations the early Christians repeated the works, even to the raising of the dead:

> . . . the miraculous cure of diseases of the most inveterate or even preternatural kind can no longer occasion any surprise, when we recollect that in the day of Irenaeus about the end of the second century, the resurrection of the dead was very far from being esteemed an uncommon event; that the miracle was frequently performed on necessary occasions, by great fasting and the joint supplication of the church of the place, and that the persons thus restored to their prayers had lived afterwards amongst them many years.[6]

The above are the words of a skeptic, Gibbon. A modern historian, Ramsay MacMullen of Yale University, in his book *Christianizing the Roman Empire, A.D. 100–400*, says that physical and mental healing must be included in any list of the causes for the new religion's rapid spread.[7] The most prevalent kind of healing that seems to be repeated in the writings of the early church fathers (these are the handful of men who left a written imprint from the end of the age of the Apostles until the official establishment of the Church in 325) was that of exorcising devils. This belief of having a devil or evil spirit within oneself can be seen in some of the New Testament healings attributed to Jesus. However, it was also a common way of speaking about any illness or discomfort that had come to "occupy" one's body.

Finally, the promise of immortality to believers was a measurable impetus to accepting the new faith. Such a hope had been lacking in the various pagan philosophies, nor had it been an explicit part of all the Judaic sects. Given the state of scientific understanding of the universe, it may have been easier for the early Christians to envision their personal immortality than it is for mankind today. On the other hand, even their Christianity had been conditioned by Greek philosophical thinking, which reinforced the concept of a soul separate from the mortal body.

Along with the spread of Christianity came the growth of organization and, not much later, of hierarchy within the organization. During the first century or so after the Apostles, the local congregations were governed by presbyters or bishops elected by the congregations. When a bishop died, a new bishop would be elected from among the presbyters, but elected by the congregation. As time went on, the bishops tended to become less the first among equals and to assert a personal authority. "The prelates of the third century imperceptibly changed the language of exhortation into that of command."[8] They also organized into regional groups, at least partly to facilitate the discussion of doctrinal issues that developed. Some bishops became more important than other bishops, and it does not take too strong an imagination to see how the race was on to become humanly important and in some degree to exercise authority over other human beings.

The final result was the establishment of a distinction between clergy and laity. Such a distinction had not existed in the pagan culture of Greece and Rome and does not appear to have been part of any plan Jesus considered. But therein lay the difficulty! Jesus himself had not actually organized a church. Yet here were his followers, trying to keep alive a vision they had received through the writings of the Apostles and by tradition.

EARLY DEVELOPMENT OF CHURCH DOCTRINE

Yale professor Jaroslav Pelikan, in his monumental six-volume work on the development of Christian doctrine entitled *The Christian*

Tradition, gives an ordered development of doctrine during the first few hundred years we are considering here. For the purposes of this book, considering whether the core of Christianity that offered men and women a spiritual home in the days of the Roman Empire is still relevant today, it is especially worth taking a look at what the early Church meant by salvation.[9] Compared to the complex discussion about the threefold Godhead that developed in the fourth century, or the nature of Christ Jesus as being both human and divine, there was relatively little discussion of the nature of the salvation Jesus accomplished. One reason for this may be that the early Church, at least for the first generation or two, expected the physical return of Jesus. This was dominant in the early preaching and was only gradually replaced by the thought that Jesus' return was either delayed or not to be expected in a literal sense. Exactly when this thought was dropped from orthodox Christian teaching is not clear.

> . . . if the teachings of the early church and of Jesus could simply be described as consistent eschatology, we could then trace the decline of such an eschatology as the primary factor in the establishment both of ecclesiastical structures and of dogmatic norms. Neither primitive Christianity nor the church catholic was consistent in so single-minded a way, as each new bit of evidence or new study of old evidence makes clear.[10]

The change was best epitomized at either extreme, Pelikan asserts, by "nothing less than the decisive shift from the categories of cosmic drama to those of being, from the Revelation of St. John the Divine to the creed of the Council of Nicea."[11] What he means by this is that the Book of Revelation represented the supposedly imminent establishment of God's kingdom after a final battle with the devil. It provides rich graphic embellishment of the final days. There are, of course, other, more metaphysical interpretations of much of John's vision. But the early Christians did expect some kind of final event to occur—quickly.

By the time we get to Nicea (A.D. 325) we arrive at the encoding of dogma that was to become essential for the Church's maintenance over the next thousand years or more.

As Christians had to cope with the idea that the return of Jesus was not imminent or, many reasoned, that they had misunderstood his teaching on this point, some developed a framework of dogma about him. As one reads about the theological arguments over the Trinity and over the nature of Jesus himself, one gains a new appreciation for the sincerity with which the early church fathers wrestled with these doctrinal questions—even if some of the wrestling, from the perspective of two thousand years, seems to have been unnecessarily complicated. The theological wrangling needs to be understood within the context in which it took place—the defense of Christianity against various forms of pagan thought and, later, against heresies within the Christian Church itself. Some of the defense also took on the coloration of the thought forms (such as Greek philosophy) to which the Church was opposed.

From the standpoint of the subject here, what is most germane is that the fathers did not directly address the content of salvation. The Nicene Creed, for instance, which was to remain a standard reference point of Christian belief, merely said that Jesus came "for the purpose of our salvation." Each of the parts of Jesus' life had some meaning for man's individual salvation: Jesus' life and teachings gave to men a new ethic of love; his passion was a kind of ransom for the sins of man (this doctrine did not emerge at first, however); and his resurrection showed the promise of eternal life.

Some of the early fathers apparently looked mainly on the first of these three aspects of Jesus' life—that it was a teaching mission. Justin Martyr spoke of Jesus that way, perhaps intending to make Jesus' message more acceptable to Greek thought, to show an affinity between the teachings of Jesus and "the aspirations of Greek philosophy."

> The divine Sower sowed his good seed throughout his creation. Justin does not make rigid and exclusive claims for divine revelation to the Hebrews so as to invalidate the value of other sources of wisdom. Abraham and Socrates are alike "Christians before Christ." But just as the aspirations of the Old Testament prophets found their fulfillment in Christ, so also the correct insights achieved by the Greek philosophers reached their completion in the gospel of Christ who embodies the highest moral ideal.[12]

This approach at that time in history did not in any way conflict with an intensity of feeling about Jesus or a weakening of commitment to his centrality in the new religion. Justin himself was willingly martyred for his beliefs. Clement of Alexandria, somewhat later, also spoke of Jesus as an example for others. Ireneus, around the year 200, also spoke of Christ as being the example for men. And "being the Logos of God, Christ was not only the example, but the exemplar and prototype of the image of God according to which man had been created."[13] Coming still later, Cyprian (200–258) told Christians "to 'imitate' what they would someday be."[14]

Much of this language is but a small step from the position Christian Science takes toward Jesus and the meaning of salvation. (These early, ante-Nicene fathers were perhaps close enough to the reality of Jesus' life not to get drawn into the theories about Jesus that developed later.) Yet official Church doctrine did not take that road in the third century. As close as the early Christians came to glimpsing the full mission of Jesus, the times were not yet ripe for teaching about the present reality of a wholly spiritual cosmos, which Jesus had fully demonstrated in his life and resurrection from the grave.

Pelikan concludes that, in spite of this reference to Jesus as example, the meaning of salvation came to lie more and more in the belief that the Christian was given an admittance into eternal life because of his beliefs. The emphasis on the Resurrection came to be identified increasingly with the meaning of salvation.

> ... when a modern western Christian turns to the Christian writers of the second and third centuries for their understanding of salvation in Christ, it is neither their attention to the teachings and example of Christ (which he may, rather superficially, identify with that of Protestant liberalism) nor their preoccupation with the passion and death of Christ (which he may, with some justification, see as an ancestor of the orthodox doctrine of vicarious atonement), but their emphasis on the saving significance of the resurrection of Christ that he will find most unusual.[15]

There is also at least the inkling that some of the Christian fathers understood this eternal life as something different from a continuation of the same kind of experience identified with life on earth. Salvation was not "simply a restoration of what had been lost in the first Adam, the original creation; it had to be an incorporation into what had been vouchsafed in the second Adam, a new creation."[16]

We may see in early Christian doctrine, then, an acceptance of Jesus' teachings as an ethical system for human relationships. There is not this early an explicit development of the idea of his death as an atonement for others' sins, but there is, most importantly, the promise of eternal life. The certainty of this promise—and they must have been aware of Paul's unequivocal statements, such as "If in this world only we have hope in Christ, we are of all men most miserable"[17]—did much to alleviate the harshness, unfairness, and inequality of life as most Christians probably experienced it. At the same time it provided a hope for the future that mankind in general had not entertained before.

Was there, in this incipient theology, any place for the concept that Jesus' example also saved man from sickness, that Jesus showed us the way to health? Since this was to become an integral part of Christian Science, and since the healings of Jesus seemed so much an integral part of the means by which he taught the way to live, one wonders just how this part of his message was continued in the first few hundred years of the religion's development.

There was indeed a place for healing in early Church doctrine. Since even a skeptic such as Gibbon seems to acknowledge that some healing continued, it would be surprising if it had been entirely omitted from the development of doctrine. It seems to have occurred most explicitly in the writings of Ireneus and Clement, both of whom are highly regarded as fathers of the early Church. Ireneus wrote that disease was one of the results of sin. It was consistent, therefore, that the same person who brought salvation to mankind should bring it health. He "insisted that the bringer of salvation from sin and the bringer of salvation from disease had to be the same."[18]

All the early church fathers were used to turning to Scripture to buttress their positions. In this case, Ireneus used the story told in Matthew 9 of Jesus healing the man who had palsy. Connecting the palsy either with some past sin of this person or perhaps only with the general human belief that man is a sinner and on that account is made to suffer, Jesus simply said to the man, "Son, be of good cheer; thy sins be forgiven thee." Somewhat later, Clement of Alexandria turned to the same Scripture as proof that "the good tutor, the Logos, healed the body and soul, granting restoration of health to the sick and forgiveness to the sinners; and to both he was 'the Savior.'"[19]

Origen, also from Alexandria, went a step farther. At the time he wrote in the third century, Origen was recognized as one of the strongest Christian theologians. He was anathematized several centuries after his death by the Council of Constantinople—in 553. Through identifying himself with Christ, he wrote, a believer would lift his human nature "to union with his divine nature and thus with God and thus to deification."[20] In this sense, Origen was the most articulate of the Eastern school of early Christian theology, a school that as a whole identified the divine spark, the Christ, as existing in every baptized Christian.

Origen exemplifies the influence the Greeks had on Christian theology. Chadwick says that, unlike some of the earlier church fathers, Origen recognized no authority in Plato. "Yet, quite unconsciously, Origen is inwardly less critical of Platonism than Clement, and proposes a system that incorporates a larger proportion of Platonic assumptions than is apparent in Clement's writings."[21] At the same time, he says, "For Origen the only source of revelation was the Bible, and he devoted many hours of each day to prayer and study, strenuously forcing himself to almost unending toil, and living with little sleep and food."[22]

Meanwhile, the Christian Church continued to grow. Some of its severest trials occurred during the last half of the third century, when there were three waves of persecution. The attempt of the theologians to give metaphysical structure to the new religion probably accounted for its growth much less than the internal cohesion and fellowship of groups of Christians trying to practice the ethic of love and compassion. The martyrdom of Christians also tended to increase the flock, although the Church was not persecuted on an Empire-wide basis until about A.D. 250. By the year 200 Christianity had made many converts among the upper classes. "The sporadic nature of persecution, which often depended on local attitudes, and the fact that before the third century the government did not take Christianity seriously, gave the Church breathing space to expand."[23]

Christianity also grew by the accretion of both Western and Oriental customs and beliefs, causing Will Durant, in his *Caesar and Christ* book, to remark that Christianity was the last great creation of the pagan world. "When Christianity conquered pagan Rome the ecclesiastical structure of the pagan church, the title and vestments of the pontifex maximus, the worship of the Great Mother and a multitude of comforting divinities, the sense of supersensible presences everywhere, the joy or solemnity of old festivals, and the pageantry of immemorial ceremony, passed like maternal blood into the new religion, and captive Rome captured her conqueror."[24]

THE GNOSTICS AS EXAMPLE OF THE ROAD NOT TAKEN

One may decry the fact that the simple religion preached by Jesus came, within a few hundred years, to be transformed into the religion of creeds, ritual, and ecclesiastical structure that was to be its main expression for over one thousand years. On the other hand, it was the Roman Catholic church that represented a civilizing and unifying presence in the Western world during the Dark and Middle Ages, and whose scholarship laid the basis for the period that was to follow the successful challenging of its monopoly of both spiritual and temporal affairs. Moreover, a great part of the Christian message on which almost all modern Christians agree—from the emphasis on love and service to others, to the overcoming of sin, to the belief in eternal life—has been consistently promulgated over the centuries.

However, we are looking here at a process of change—how the unorganized followers of Jesus, trying to emulate the ideals of the Sermon on the Mount and the healing practice of Jesus, became within a few generations first a vital movement able to impart its sense of the Christian promise to others, and then both a spiritual and a temporal power able to wield its authority over much of the world. Any high school student of history knows the rough outline of Western history, and the role that the Church has played in it. But what if the Church had not developed into the combined temporal and spiritual power it grew into? It is time here to pay special attention to the concerns of one element of the early Christian movement that later came to be considered heretical—the gnostics. And, to begin with, let us remember that they were judged as heretics only in retrospect by those who, by virtue of "winning," became the representatives and definers of orthodoxy.

The gnostics are not susceptible of easy definition. Part of the problem with them is that by nature they were what the theologians call syncretistic. That is, they were not a group with a unified system of beliefs that one can put into a simple definition. Another part of the problem is that gnosticism in one sense has never entirely left the Church.

While not easy to define because of their own diversity, gnostics tended to agree above all that one could find the divine within. In other words, one could directly experience God's presence. On the one hand, this is what perhaps most Christians believe they achieve through prayer. On the other, it can lead to a kind of mysticism that is more akin to what Westerners think of as part of the Oriental mind, a submergence of individuality into some cosmic whole. But one Catholic theologian says that gnosticism in some form continued in the Catholic church well into the thirteenth century.[25]

As one movement among several that were later treated as heresies, the gnostics are not as important in the development of early Christianity as the attention given them here. The reason for the attention is that the gnostic movement illustrates issues that, like an underground stream, would surface periodically. They would come up again during the Protestant Reformation, and they were clearly issues that Mrs. Eddy confronted head on. At the same time, they deserve more attention than they would get if treated as simply one more heresy in the Church. For the gnostic movement did not spring up several centuries after orthodox Christian doctrine had become established. The gnostics were there from the start, and it was the rejection of their views that helped define orthodoxy. One writer, Walter Bauer, even suggests that "perhaps—I repeat, perhaps—certain manifestations of Christian life that the authors of the church renounce as 'heresies' originally had not been such at all, but, at least here and there, were the only forms of the new religion; that is, for those regions, they were simply 'Christianity.'"[26] This view is expressed in another form by the eminent Harvard professor of New Testament, Helmut Koester, in his just published book, *Ancient Christian Gospels*, where he writes, "Diversity rather than unity is the hallmark of the beginning of the traditions about Jesus."[27]

There are several ways in which the gnostic movement might be treated. I have chosen to bring up four points here; the reasons for their inclusion and their order will be seen as we discuss them here and, even more particularly, when we come to the metaphysical system of Christian Science.

1. The gnostics had a deep conviction about the primacy of spiritual reality. Whether or not God had created the material universe, they saw it as secondary to their vision of the spiritual.

2. Their vision of an essentially spiritual reality apart from the material led them to state the question about man's redemption differently from the orthodox position. Instead of a model that eventually defined orthodoxy in terms of sin, forgiveness, and atonement, they saw individual redemption as releasing a person from the illusion of identification with the material.

3. Because they stated the terms of man's salvation differently from orthodoxy, it necessarily followed that they viewed the life and works of Jesus in a different manner.

4. If salvation became wholly an individual matter, the church must play a less decisive role in the life of the Christian than it did in orthodoxy. Many gnostic teachers emphasized that each person must play an active role in finding the divine within. This emphasis tended to sweep aside such orthodox concerns as ritual and the sacraments.

1. The Material Universe

Western thought has accepted a dichotomy between mind and matter that separates it from Eastern philosophies. The Western tradition begins with Plato's idealism, in which a world of ideas stands behind the material. Not quite the same concept, but in modern times philosophers have lived for a long time with Descartes's division of the world into subjects and objects.

In the Bible and particularly in the New Testament, there is the contrast between the material and the spiritual. The Jewish tradition was not as explicit on the subject, but the thought was still there. Texts such as "he uttered his voice; the earth melted"[28] surely suggested the impermanence of material things and the enduring nature of what belongs to God. And many of the Old Testament stories indicated the might of intelligence, of God-derived guidance, or what appeared to be outright intervention with material process to supersede the laws of a material universe. In much of the Old Testament, the good life is described as one overflowing with the abundance of material possessions—the barns filled with plenty, the presses bursting with new wine.

When we come to the instructions of Jesus, on the other hand, the emphasis changes from the evidence of material abundance to the presence of spiritual qualities. Although Jesus promised his followers that they would receive all they needed from following God first, the Christian promise is always within the context of "A man's life consisteth not in the abundance of things which he possesseth."[29] The tangible benefits one can expect from following the Master were summed up by Paul in his letter to the Galatians: "The fruit of the Spirit is love, joy, peace, longsuffering, gentleness, goodness, faith, meekness, temperance."[30]

This shift from an emphasis on the material to the spiritual does not necessarily imply a distrust of the structure of the material universe. But that is what at least some of the gnostics believed. Did they get these beliefs from an acquaintance with Neoplatonic phi-losophy? Or from Oriental philosophies? Or did they believe them to have emanated from the teachings of Jesus himself?

In the words of a Protestant critic of the gnostics, they believed that "the cosmos is an abortion; humanity, in the fleshly sense, along with all materiality, is a mistake."[31] For those who still take the sto-ries of creation in the Book of Genesis as being literally true, this would be tantamount to turning one's back on the creation God had made. Actually, while some of the more radical gnostics believed that the material universe was *not* of God's invention, the more general gnostic belief was that God had allowed some lesser power to make the material universe in order to put man on some kind of "learning curve" to find the more important spiritual reality.

If the material universe is some lesser form of reality, then it is but a step to believing that the external events that transpire in it are of no intrinsic importance. Was this step in line with anything Jesus had preached, or was it an inheritance from Eastern philosophies about which something was known at that time?

Whatever the sources of the belief, Elaine Pagels, in her book *The Gnostic Gospels*, says:

> . . . orthodox tradition implicitly affirms bodily experience as the central fact of human life. What one does physically—one eats and drinks, engages in sexual life or avoids it, saves one's life or gives it up—all are vital elements in one's religious development. But those gnostics who regarded the essential part of every person as the "inner spirit" dismissed such physical experience, pleasurable or painful, as a distraction from spiritual reality—indeed, as an illusion. No wonder, then, that far more people identified with the orthodox portrait than with the "bodiless spirit" of gnostic tradition.[32]

The gnostic Christians tended to think of evil less in the traditional Old Testament sense of personal moral lapse than in terms of anguish over the entire human condition. One of the gnostic texts, which did not get included in the New Testament, is entitled the Gospel of Truth. It talks about the "anguish and terror" of the human condition, "as if lost in a fog or haunted in sleep by terrifying nightmares."[33]

"Since such experiences," says Pagels, "especially the fear of death and dissolution, are located, in the first place, in the body, the gnostic tended to mistrust the body, regarding it as the saboteur that inevitably engages him in suffering."[34] This distrust was then extended to a similar attitude toward the entire universe.

> If "the many"—the unenlightened people—believed that they would find fulfillment in family life, sexual relationships, business, politics, ordinary employment or leisure, the gnostic

rejected this belief as illusion. Some radicals rejected all trans-
actions involving sexuality or money.[35]

The gnostic attitude toward sex was ambiguous. While most
gnostics lived lives of personal asceticism and self-denial, their ene-
mies claimed that at least some of them occasionally indulged in sexual orgies as a kind of cathartic. One must add the cautionary note that
much information written by the gnostics themselves has become
available only in the last two decades; more may still come to light.
Thus their history is, in a very real sense, in the process of being
rewritten. Moreover, many of the writings against the gnostics were
authored by the church fathers, and not all of what they said in regard
to a subject so fraught with peril as a discussion of someone else's sexuality can be assumed to have been entirely accurate. (One may also
recall the many references to fornication in Paul's letters, which indicate that sexual morality was as much a problem then as now, and that
chastity for the unmarried and fidelity for the married was expected
of the Christian.)

What is abundantly clear is that the gnostics rejected the world of
material appearance. Whether this led them to ignore the material
world or to try to transform it through their individual faith is less
clear.

Rejecting the world of material appearance does not actually
tell us anything unless we know what action followed from this rejection. Pagels suggests that the gnostics might have carried on the
Christian tradition of healing better or longer than did the more
orthodox Christians, but the available evidence to this effect is
somewhat ambiguous. The legendary stories about Thecla, a young
woman who chose asceticism as a way of life and followed Paul,
include her reputation as a healer. It is unclear, however, whether
Thecla should herself be considered a gnostic.[36]

The gnostic scriptures themselves contain a variety of texts. Some
are pre-Christian in origin, and not all of them written after the time
of Jesus take his life or words as their starting point. It would be difficult to gain from them alone a sense of where a gnostic stood. There
is, however, enough uniformity in them to suggest that the gnostics

believed that God in the sense Christians approach God—an almighty, perfect power—could not have created the material universe, with its manifest evil and changeability. They explained matter, however, as coming at the end of a chain of "emanations" from God. A hierarchy of creative powers was positioned, as it were, between God and the material universe, which finally resulted in a lesser power that could create the material universe. The gnostic myths about material creation seem, to one first reading them, even more complicated than the stories accompanying Greek and Roman mythology, although this impression is undoubtedly heightened by their unfamiliarity. On the face of it, the gnostics' position would seem to confirm the material universe, although not of God's creation. Such a position does not lead to the kind of dominion over material conditions that characterized Jesus' healings of disease, his multiplication of food, and his walking on the water or stilling the tempest.

2. The Nature of Salvation

We have seen that the concept of salvation was not well articulated during the first three centuries of the Christian era. It did, however, include the ethical approach epitomized by the Beatitudes and the entire Sermon on the Mount, and had as its most attractive feature the promise of eternal life and the equality of all men in the eyes of God.

It is not at all clear that the gnostics disagreed with any of the above. However, the first item on the gnostic agenda dealing with salvation would have had to do with clearing away the sense of the material universe. Man could not find his permanent home in the universe that the physical senses describe. Philip Lee, a Presbyterian cleric in Nova Scotia, has written at length about the gnostics (and without, I should add, admiration for what he regards as their escapism). In these sentences he catches some of what the gnostic position regarding salvation was:

> In gnostic thought, insofar as a person is spirit (pneuma), that person realizes that he or she does not belong to the cosmos. The pneuma originated or eternally existed in a transcendent

world. There will be no consolation for the pneuma, no relief
for the intense nostalgia for "home," so long as the pneuma
remains in this abyss called cosmos.[37]

Lee then quotes Goethe's hero Faust on this dichotomy between
the two views of man's nature:

> Two souls alas! are dwelling in my breast,
> And each is fain to leave its brother.
> The one, fast clinging, to the world adheres
> With clutching organs, in love's sturdy lust;
> The other strongly lifts itself from dust
> To yonder high, ancestral spheres.[38]

One could with even greater relevance quote Jesus, again in his talk
with Nicodemus, when he said: "That which is born of the flesh is
flesh; and that which is born of the Spirit is spirit. Marvel not that
I said unto thee, Ye must be born again."[39]

To say that the cosmos, or material world, was itself what one must
overcome could be to undertake a lifelong pilgrimage to rise above
the material sense of creation, exchanging it for a spiritual view. We
shall be more specific about this approach when taking up the theological position of Christian Science. Or, conversely, it could
mean being insufficiently concerned with human morality to take the
corrective steps one could to redeem even this limited material sense
of things. Gnosticism's critics claimed that it took the latter approach
and was, in effect, escapist in its attitude toward present existence.
While gnosticism may not have had a fair hearing, this charge that
the gnostics ignored evil in their attempt to reach the "high, ancestral spheres" cannot be disregarded.[40]

Some of the criticism of the gnostics' approach to salvation was
almost surely based on false impressions. Pagels notes that the
gnostics "came to the conviction that the only way out of suffering
was to realize the truth about humanity's place and destiny in the universe."[41] So far, so good. This really does not sound different from
the statement of Jesus in the Gospel of John: "Ye shall know the truth,
and the truth shall make you free."

It was the means of knowing the truth that created the tension between the gnostics and the budding Church hierarchy. For, how does one know the truth? Individually. "Convinced that the only answers were to be found within, the gnostic engaged on an intensely private interior journey."[42] If salvation really does consist in knowing the truth about something, then it can be learned only by each individual at his or her own pace. This is not to say that the Christian life can be practiced in isolation, since moral and ethical positions acquire meaning only as they are expressed in actual relationships with others.

The gnostics evidently went it alone, and for that they were criticized. Rev. Lee writes, "The solitary nature of the religious quest is a continuing theme of gnostic literature. At times its peculiar thrust would seem to require a serious adjustment of the biblical tradition."[43] He gives as an example the saying of Jesus in Matthew, "Where two or three are gathered in my name, I am with them."[44] To the contrary, some gnostic literature has Jesus saying, "Wheresoever there be two, they are not without God; and wherever there is one alone, I say, I am with him."[45] This seemed to make communion with or worship of God on a one-to-one basis preferable to even a small community of followers.

It should not be surprising that the modern-day Swiss psychoanalyst C. G. Jung, who considered himself in the Christian tradition, should have felt similarly to the gnostics. In a conversation he had with his informal biographer, Laurens van der Post, he referred to the same remark of Jesus. The implication van der Post got from the conversation was that Jung thought that two or three were perhaps the *maximum* number who could come together to profitably learn of God instead of the minimum, as most readers of the New Testament have long assumed. But since the analyst-patient relationship is also basically one of the individual's learning who he is (although not on the same philosophic ground as the Christian), one can see why Jung would have sympathized with the gnostics' individual search for the truth.[46]

3. Christ Jesus as Savior

Let us sum up the gnostic position thus far. First, the material universe is secondary and in some sense flawed. God is not responsible for the flaws and sufferings of this life. Second, because this flaw of materiality is basic to everything mortals are involved in, salvation consists in escaping from, or rising above, this universe, which is characterized by suffering. Leaving aside the question of whether the gnostics gave enough attention to personal morality, moral perfection alone does not sum up the content of salvation. One must learn the truth about man and the universe, and although this truth might not be expressed in precise enough terms (at least at the time of the gnostics), it had something to do with the permanence of spiritual reality versus the transitory nature of the material universe.

Given this viewpoint, the gnostic did not see Jesus as a personal savior. Those gnostic texts or scriptures that do deal specifically with Jesus, such as the Gospel of Truth and the Gospel of Thomas, show him as pointing the way to the truth but not *being* the only way himself. In this respect, the gnostics diverged from all Christian orthodoxy, Protestant as well as Roman Catholic, until the spread of Unitarian doctrine in the eighteenth and nineteenth centuries. The search for truth was so intensely individual that the gnostics could not see the example of Jesus' life as the demonstration of Truth itself. However, the sayings that the gnostic texts attribute to Jesus are believable as being uttered by him. In the Gospel of Thomas, Jesus says, "When you come to know yourselves, then you will become known."

The orthodox approach could not tolerate this gnostic sense that self-knowledge was the way of salvation. Orthodoxy was already well down the road of self-denial as the route to salvation. Now, it is possible that semantics has a role to play in understanding this controversy. There may actually be a considerable overlap in the two concepts of self-knowledge and self-denial. But if the search for the self is selfish, if it only involves digging to the core of a human psyche that is unconnected to any thing or power outside itself, it is a fruitless search. It is essentially the position of the egotist. On the other hand, if in searching for the self one actually means he is looking beyond or behind the ephemeral, the passing, maybe even the material, to what is enduring about man, it could be that in finding *that* man he does find the link with the divine. Even then, of course, the search would be sweeter and shorter if one could begin with God, and from there learn what man must be if he is linked to God.

Now, this *may* be what at least some of the gnostics were trying to do. Their language may have lent itself too easily to misrepresentation. (Their individual search for salvation was also so opposed to the developing structure of a universal church that there may have been some willful "miscasting" of the gnostic position by orthodoxy in later years.) Or, they may simply have been on the wrong path. Whichever is the case, they looked to Jesus as one who had given them important clues in their search. There is no evidence that they looked to him as unique in history, however, or to the actual events of his life—his birth, crucifixion, and resurrection—as events that of themselves revealed something about the real man. Some of their writings would lead one to think that they did not believe in his physical resurrection. At least as far as the gnostic writings that have been uncovered so far would show, Jesus would not appear to have a unique role in human history, and therefore no essential, irreplaceable part in man's salvation.

This point is made here and will be reiterated later in the discussion of Christian Science. At many points Mrs. Eddy seems to have reached conclusions that have some analogies to gnostic positions (as in the nature of the material universe or in understanding salvation as knowledge). On the question of the incarnation, however, even though she did not follow the concept of the orthodox Christian Trinity, her position on Jesus is far removed from the vague position he occupies in the gnostic teachings.

4. *The Role of the Church*

If salvation is entirely individual, the formal church organization would not be as essential as it was to become for later generations of orthodox Christians. Yet the genius of the early church fathers was to organize a universal church. Probably no lesser, loosely organized church would have withstood the Dark Ages that followed the fall of Rome. "While the gnostic saw himself as 'one out of a thousand, two out of ten thousand,' the orthodox experienced himself as one member of a universal church."[47] This membership in an organization that taught him the rules of conduct for daily living, that regulated family life and gave sanctity to the human entrance and exit from life, was an enduring part of Western civilization during a thousand years when it might have seemed that civilization was slipping permanently backward.

Raised in the United States, I was used to seeing large Catholic churches crowded onto city street corners—such as St. Patrick's Cathedral in New York. But to experience the thrust of the Gothic spires in even smaller European cities was an entirely different matter. One of my strongest visual memories of Europe goes back to the first time my wife and I approached Chartres cathedral. It was the Christmas season. The dark winter sky hung over all of France, it seemed, and as we approached the town of Chartres through the bare wheat fields, there we saw looming high above the modest houses of the town the grand cathedral that had taken two hundred years to complete. I knew what its windows looked like from art books I had studied. But to see their grandeur in the midst of the fairly humble town of Chartres, one could not help but sense some part of the strength of the faith that had built that cathedral over several generations—and the role of that faith in building a sense of Europe over more than a thousand years.

As we have seen in chapter 2, such was not the American experience except in the very early years of the Puritan settlements. Partly because religious life is so fragmented in the United States, the gnostic position about church does not strike us as being as strange as it seemed to their opponents at the time. The gnostics saw the church as essentially a voluntary, spiritual association. Since salvation consisted in gaining a personal acquaintance with God, the church could not by definition be the vehicle for that process to occur. Moreover, since the gnostics believed that such acquaintance was fairly rare and gained only by the few, it was actually abhorrent to them to see vast numbers of people counted as Christians who knew little about the demands of Christianity. The Second Treatise of the Great Seth says:

> We were hated and persecuted, not only by those who are ignorant [pagans], but by those who think they are advancing the name of Christ, since they were unknowingly empty, not knowing who they are, like dumb animals.[48]

The "visible community" calling itself a church was not their concept of church. To them, the right concept of church had nothing to do with organization and the hierarchy of the clergy, but with "the level of understanding of its members, and the quality of their relationship with one another."[49]

Pagels cites Hippolytus, who was at first among the orthodox but later became a gnostic, as complaining that "the majority of 'self-professed Christians' were incapable of living up to the standard of the true church, which consisted of the 'community of those who live in holiness.'"[50]

Another orthodox Christian, Tertullian, at first wrote polemics against the gnostics. When he later broke with orthodoxy, he also conceived of a kind of "spiritual church" in which only its members recognized who the other members were.

If church as an institution was not essential to man's salvation, what then was there to hold it together? This has been the problem many Protestant communities have faced since the time of Martin Luther. The closer the church approximates a spiritual community, one may argue that it carries little weight within a society composed of other institutions. Yet to many Christians, the institutional aspects of church too easily overburden the spiritual element that is the church's purpose.

The critics of the gnostics saw their view toward an organized, hierarchical church as one more bit of evidence of their innate egotism and unconcern for their fellowman. Philip Lee figures that gnostic thinking probably progressed something like this:

> . . . as the Christian Church became universally accepted by the masses, its preaching adapted to the general public and its worship sometimes pro forma, the more enlightened Christians began to yearn for a kind of faith which was more intense, more spiritual—which called for more dedication. These persons were offended by being put in the same category with ordinary Christians who were operating on so low a level of intellect and spirit.[51]

That kind of description sounds plausible; it also sounds egotistical on the part of the gnostics at first hearing. However, to those who seek the way through an understanding of the life and works of Christ Jesus, being a Christian is hard and demanding, albeit rewarding, work. The very idea that Christianity could, within so short a time frame, be "universally accepted by the masses" would strike such serious Christians as an impossibility. This view is reinforced by the fact that so much of the nominally Christian populations of North Africa and the Middle East were converted to Islam in the seventh century.

Whether the gnostics actually promoted themselves as either an intellectual or a spiritual elite is unclear. It is possible that those who were offended by the gnostics' independence found it convenient to pin the derogatory label of a spiritual elite on them. Moreover, since the church was in the process of locating all ecclesiastical authority under its wings, it would have been understandable for it to try to stamp out even a loose movement of people who believed they were getting their insights directly from God. The church was also trying to define Christianity in a still hostile political environment while the gnostic movement was at its height during the second half of the second century. The eventual adoption of a creed made it simple to define who was "in" and who was "out" of the church.

The Montanists, another heresy, which eventually was to claim Tertullian's allegiance, believed in the possibility of continuing revelation—as have others all the way down to Ralph Waldo Emerson. And Christian Scientists today, as we shall see, while regarding their religion as a restoration of primitive Christianity, look on its metaphysical statement as a present-day revelation to Mrs. Eddy.

A side question that remains unanswered is whether the gnostics self-indulged in a kind of secret knowledge that they egotistically hid from others, or whether the gnosis (a Greek word for knowledge) they stood for merely represented the different kinds of knowing for which we use different verbs in some foreign languages. There is *wissen* (German) and *savoir* (French) for knowing a fact, *kennen* and *connaître* for being acquainted with, having intimate knowledge of someone, and so on. Was the gnostic merely saying that he had a kind of knowledge of God that could not be expressed by the intellect? Was he saying that he had an experience that transcended the ability of the human intellect to put into verbal forms? These questions admittedly tilt in the direction of the gnostics; yet it seems dangerous to accept without questioning the general reputation the gnostics have had for two millennia when their history has been interpreted largely by those who had triumphed over them.

* * *

To speak of "triumph" is probably a misnomer. The beliefs of the gnostics were inimical to an organized, hierarchical church, but it was inevitable that organization would win in any battle with "dis"-organization. The gnostics did not shun association with each other, but because of the syncretistic nature of their beliefs, they had no need to unite in creeds or argue with those they disagreed with. Given the centuries of turmoil and relative darkness that were about to descend on most of the Western world, the groups of gnostics would have been further fragmented and decimated.

The Roman Catholic church acculturated itself by the accretion of many rituals and customs from the pagan Mediterranean world. This strengthened its appeal to the average person and in fact made it easier to leave the pagan world for what was nominally Christian. The church had become so well organized by the time Rome fell (a full century and a half after Constantine had made Christianity the official religion of the Empire) that it not only could withstand the ages that followed, but would itself become the symbol of the civilization that replaced the Roman Empire.

What is most important in this discussion are not the gnostics themselves, but to understand that the questions they raised would come back for new answers at a later time. As Chadwick says, "Most of the main issues then faced by the church in its formative period have remained virtually permanent questions in Christian history—questions which receive an answer but are then reiterated in a modified shape in each age."[52] For Christian Scientists, the four topics just discussed have more significance for the age in which we live than do some of the questions of dogma (such as the Trinity) that became the topics of several later church councils.

Whether the gnostics were clear about the reality of matter does not really concern us today. But if mankind at large was and still is confused as to the existence of a spiritual universe, this does have a major bearing on the definition of salvation. If salvation is in the first instance a matter of direct acquaintance with God, it has to be based on some kind of knowledge and not on mere believing. Such knowledge may be defined in a different manner than the knowledge we get from books. The human mind of itself may well be incapable of achieving it, but the search would still be an individual one.

The gnostic movement also raised important questions about the nature of Jesus and his role in the individual's salvation. Some gnostic writings seem to deny the human side of Jesus—such as the fact that he actually suffered as a human being on the cross. While they did see his life as some kind of example, they missed the fact that almost all Christians, whatever their doctrinal disagreements, have agreed on—the centrality of Jesus as the supreme figure in human history. In this area, while Christian Science differs from Christian orthodoxy quite sharply in its verbalisms about Jesus, its position is actually very close in meaning to that of the major Christian tradition. A gnostic would not have written, as Mary Baker Eddy did, "The cross is the central emblem of history."[53]

As for church, one can have great sympathy for the gnostics. They did not see the herd of mankind all becoming Christian at once. Nor, in practice, did the orthodox, for the separation into clergy and laity and the eventual establishment of religious orders indicated that the orthodox also recognized that not all Christians were equally deep in their study and practice.

The gnostics' association with each other on a voluntary basis seems to stand much closer to the kind of societies that first sprang up after the time of Jesus. That these alone would not have been enough to account for the spread of Christianity is partly a commentary on the nature of the times. However, the organization of churches whose sacraments actually became a prerequisite for salvation was a giant step from the simple kind of religious meetings the early Christians had had (which, as noted earlier, were modeled closely on the pattern of the Jewish synagogue).

As we shall see in the final chapter, the model on which the future of Christian Science rests is a local democratic organization, with no distinction whatsoever between clergy and laity. There is, in fact, no clergy. The evolution of the Protestant churches to the ultimate form of democracy required two things: first, an evolution in thinking about the nature of church from an agency that itself provided salvation and enforced the rules leading to it to a voluntary association of all those who were working out their salvation in a similar manner; and second, a kind of societal commitment to the values of democracy in which each church member recognized his responsibility to the group by supporting the minimal but important functions that the church alone can provide the community. Such a voluntary association can function and prosper only to the extent that its members consistently exhibit a high degree of love and selflessness toward each other and their communities. This, as those who today try to practice Christianity within their churches of whatever denomination know, is itself a challenge to grow in Christian grace. It is no small wonder that such a form of church organization could not succeed in the times of the Roman Empire. It is a wonder that something approaching the democracy of the members should even have been attempted by any of the early Christians.

Chapter 5

THE NATURE OF DISCOVERY

The opening chapter asked but did not try to answer the questions: Why are discoveries generally made by individuals? Why do at least some discoveries take a long period of time before they are adopted by the very people who would get the most benefit from them? We live in an age of continuing discovery and invention, yet few of us have probably ever thought much about the process of discovery itself.

Before considering Mary Baker Eddy's discovery of Christian Science, it would be helpful to introduce two very basic concepts about discovery: one, that discoveries are generally made by individuals; and two, that the process does have a rational explanation—even if few of us enter the ranks of discoverers or inventors ourselves. And that explanation tends to lie more in the direction of hard work and dedication than in the concept of a bolt out of the blue.

Explaining the process of discovery is not to engage in some kind of psychological reductionism. It is, rather, to explain what elements need to be present for the process of discovery to work. Now, the discoveries we are most apt to be familiar with are those in the area of the physical and biological sciences. I ask the reader to withhold judgment at this point if he or she wonders how the word *discovery* can be applied to a religion. This chapter should make that bridge possible in the reader's mind. But there are clearly differences between a discovery in the physical sciences and one that applies to a religion, since by its nature a religion takes in the entire panorama of human life—one's value system, individual goals in life, and view of the outside world. Thus, one would naturally expect that any religion claiming to have a radically new view of the nature of reality, or of the basis for human relationships and values, and particularly of the relationship of one's health to one's thinking, would by those very facts take considerably longer to be accepted or adopted by a large proportion of mankind than would be a discrete set of equations in physics that was susceptible of relatively easy verification.

The following pages will, I hope, validate Mrs. Eddy's contention that Christian Science came about as a discovery in much the same way that other advances in the sciences have occurred. She also wished Christian Science to be *judged* as a science, since it would stand the test of time only if it could be practiced as reliably as a science can be. Furthermore, its establishment as a science explains why, even though it is foremost a religion, its proselytizing has been more in the general nature of making information about it available than in trying to cajole or convince someone into only passively accepting the claims it makes about its usefulness.

When I mention Christian Science to an acquaintance, one reaction that I have become used to is, "I wouldn't have expected to have the word *science* connected to a religion." Christian Scientists are accustomed to this initial response and, while there are varying dictionary definitions of "science," perhaps we can apply it here in the sense of a way of doing something—in this case, how to practice the Christianity of Christ Jesus. Several of the examples of discovery in this chapter deal with the most famous steps in man's discovery of his physical environment, or with modern technologies that have sprung from basic scientific discovery.

It may seem inappropriate to someone whose entire world is explained for him by a rational, materially scientific viewpoint even to speak of scientific discoveries in conjunction with Mrs. Eddy's discovery of Christian Science. To such a reader I would say two things: first, the application of any system of thought that touches on every aspect of life, that engages the human consciousness in every decision it makes, is clearly not as precisely described as a chemical or physical reaction. Every human being comes to life with a different background and predisposition. What each person does with his or her religion will be unique to that person. Second, for someone whose entire world is explained by the cosmology of today's physical scientist, there is little more to be said. For many of us, though, and that includes many leading physical scientists, there is that quality of spirituality without which life is not lived to the fullest. Until there is a place in the great equation that explains the yearning many feel for spirituality and the effects in their lives when they have found it, there is still room for discovery.

DISCOVERY AND THE INDIVIDUAL;
HOW A PARADIGM CHANGES

The most exciting part of the concept of discovery is the thought that it makes apparent something that was already there. Analogies abound. Imagine Columbus looking for a continent to the west (even though he found not India but only the West Indies) and seeing birds in the air the day before landfall. It was there, but Columbus was almost alone at that point in believing that his ship would in fact find the continent. Or imagine Albert Einstein working in the patent office in Zurich and developing the mathematical formula that became the theory of general relativity. The relationships it describes had been there all the time, but his inquiring mind was the first to uncover them.

Many readers will be familiar with current theories about the brain, which explain that the left half of the brain thinks in linear fashion, memorizes, and so on, while the right half of the brain thinks conceptually. Acts of creation, the ability to get the "big picture," are alleged to proceed from this imaginative side of the brain. But this much said, very little or even nothing has been explained as to why so few of us do anything that can be thought of as a lasting discovery.

A medical doctor, Richard Bergland, writing about a new theory regarding the structure of the human brain, has addressed this issue of discovery. He makes the point, first of all, that discoveries are almost always made by individuals and not by committees. In describing the process of discovery, he says:

> Along each path intellectual base camps have been constructed by teams of climbers who decided it was a propitious time to break camp and move to a higher place. Few if any of these new base camps were found by teams of scouts; most of the upward steps were taken first by people acting alone. . . . The dents in the frontiers of science, the new paradigms, have almost always been made by lone scouts.[1]

In most of what we do, we require a pattern. Even in activities that involve independent thinking or action, we organize life into modules. In some of them, independent thinking takes place; and in others, activities are more by rote and can be accomplished by whole groups of people.

In the sciences, all knowledge is organized. The pattern of organization is referred to as a paradigm, another word for a model. It is only because we have agreed upon models for the different branches of knowledge that we are able to communicate with one another about them. One analogy that might serve as an example is that we would have no common way of finding the same word in a dictionary if all the words weren't first arranged according to an agreed-upon order of the alphabet.

Knowledge fits into categories; bits are related. For those working in a special field, one partial explanation for the possibility of discovery is that bits of information are found that do not fit into the known or accepted patterns. Some of the words in our make-believe dictionary have letters that were not in the alphabet with which we started. Someone who is not "ready" to make the new discovery may continue to try to fit the bits of information into the old pattern, and it may even appear that they do fit. Then comes one of these people who is the scout, ready to break camp and find higher ground—a new paradigm—and he introduces the new paradigm. Thomas Kuhn, in *The Structure of Scientific Revolutions*, published in the early 1960s and now a classic on the subject, writes:

Men whose research is based on shared paradigms are committed to the same rules and standards for scientific practice. . . . scientific revolutions are inaugurated by a growing sense
that an existing paradigm has ceased to function adequately in
the exploration of an aspect of nature.[2]

All of this leads up to Bergland's own concern that the existing
paradigm about the human brain, mainly that it functions as a kind
of supercomputer, is grossly inadequate. He goes on to detail his theory that the brain is better described as a large gland. That is not the
subject of this piece, although Bergland's theory is apropos of this
book in one sense. The dichotomy between mind and matter that
permeates Western thought is somewhat changed if the brain is seen
as even less differentiated in nature from the rest of the human body.
(It can still perform a unique function.)[3]

If thought in any field accepts a false paradigm, or model, all the
work done in that field will continue to be flawed to some extent until
a better—or even the correct—paradigm is discovered. Bergland follows this argument through to set up his own theory about the nature
of the brain, and he uses as illustration the false concept about the
circulation of the blood that existed throughout the Middle Ages and
even beyond. It is useful in terms of this book because, in the light
of Christian Science, certain false paradigms also existed during the
same period that blurred the real significance of the life of Christ
Jesus for the rest of mankind in all ages.

The discovery that blood circulates and that the heart is the
organ that controls this circulation was made by Sir William Harvey
in 1628. Yet, a Greek physician, Galen, had come very close to making the same discovery fifteen hundred years earlier. Galen, however,
was working with some false paradigms. His work as a doctor
should have convinced him that much of what he accepted and even
promoted was false.

To the ancient Greeks, everything in the universe was composed
of only four elements—fire, air, water, and earth. By the time of
Galen, the concept of humors in the body as sources of disease had
become widely accepted. Galen developed a theory of four different
humors in the body, each of which supposedly had a discrete effect.

The theory coincided neatly with the Greek concept of four elements. To describe the action of these supposed humors, it was necessary for him to invent several anatomical myths, which, Bergland says, as a doctor he must have known were not true.

> Galen wrote 22,000 pages of descriptive anatomy; he was no amateur anatomist. Yet to serve his paradigm he literally poked the body full of holes that didn't exist.[4]

His mistake pleased the chemists, philosophers, theologians, astrologers, and physicians of his day, according to Bergland. It did not ruffle any of the paradigms in their respective fields. Yet, through his dissection of bodies, Galen (let us remember that he was the most famous physician of his age and the personal physician to the Roman emperor Marcus Aurelius) had come within earshot of "hearing" that the blood circulates in the body. Instead, by bending what he had observed to make it fit the existing paradigm, he delayed medical knowledge in that area for another fifteen hundred years. "Both the Christian and the Islamic religions helped to ensure the passage of Galen's [mistake] for seventy generations. Both religions maintained that Galen had given the world the 'truth' about the body; it was written in his words, and pictures were not needed."[5]

I find this example of Galen particularly germane because of the time period it covers. Someone hearing in the twentieth century for the first time about Christian Science as a new discovery might very well be skeptical as to how anything new about Christianity could have been discovered so late in the Christian era. One reason for this skepticism would be that we are tempted to believe that all conceptual developments have moved in the past just a little slower than today. We are aware, of course, that things move faster now. In fact, the pace of invention quickens with each generation. More scientists are alive today than have been alive in all former periods.

The reality about the pace of change is that it has so quickened that we have little concept at all of how difficult it once was to dislodge any entrenched idea. For one thing, before the age of printing with movable type (Gutenberg's Bible is 1453), only a very few people were able to read books in a very few libraries. One had to be extremely rich to have a personal library. Almost all knowledge was passed down orally. One knew only what he could remember. We are probably unable even to conceive of the mental patterns that existed for all but a very small elite before the beginning of the sixteenth century.

Now, the patterns existing in one discipline differ from those in another. Lack of medical instrumentation, along with a disinclination to look for more answers in the human body itself, delayed the advance of medicine during the Middle Ages. In the case of religion and philosophy, the dominance of the Roman Catholic church as both a religious and a temporal power exercised a kind of thought control over religious matters for about the same fifteen hundred years that Galen's theories prevailed in medicine.

Even the Protestant Reformation did not question the basic tenets of Christianity as they had existed since about A.D. 300. Most of the Reformation dealt with the authority of the church over the individual, including the role of the church as an institution through which one gained salvation. Some of the Protestant denominations that began at the time of the Reformation in each country of Europe, besides breaking with the ecclesiastical monopoly claimed by Rome, did not see the nature of church as a mediatorial instrument of salvation in the same way Catholicism had defined it. Beyond that, there were some substantial differences among the Protestants themselves.

Yet, to go back to our earlier discussion of the issues involved in the gnostic heresy, none of the major denominations to come into being asked the key questions that the gnostics had asked. The nature of reality was not disturbed. The role of Jesus as personal exemplar and not mainly a divine being was not questioned. (The Unitarian church, which would become known mainly in the United States in the nineteenth century, actually had its beginnings in the sixteenth in Europe. One early Unitarian, Servetus, was burned at the stake in 1560 for rejecting the divinity of Jesus. The church got its main start in what is now Moldavia.)

In terms of historic time, the time lapse between Luther nailing his theses on the church door in Wittenberg in 1517 and Mrs. Eddy's discovery of Christian Science in 1866 is not all that long—some 350 years, as opposed to the twelve hundred years that it took to challenge the exclusivity of the Roman church.

The thinking that probably prevails among Protestants is that the relative freedom of religious inquiry that existed in many of the major Protestant denominations would have yielded up any new fruit long before 1866, if indeed there were any new insights to be found. One says "relative freedom" because, among the major Protestant groups, the Bible remained the sole authority of Christian revelation, and interpretation of the Bible was still not in the hands of each believer. Given the mind-set regarding the nature of creation (of reality), of man and his alleged fall in the Garden of Eden, and of the role of Jesus as personal savior, it would take still another revolution in thought to get back to the basic questions that had been matters of disagreement in the three hundred years following the time of Christ.

One summer in the early 1950s, when I was new to Christian Science, I decided to visit a large Presbyterian church on the Gold Coast of Chicago. One of my uncles had been a member there. He had passed on suddenly when I was a small boy, and I still remembered the young minister holding me on his knee and talking with me. A cousin had been married in that church. I felt more or less at home. So imagine my surprise when in the middle of a sermon I no longer remember, this same minister began to speak against new interpretations of Christianity. It was impossible, he said, that anyone would have anything new to say; this had all been worked out at the time of the Reformation by church scholars. Satisfaction with an existing paradigm is not, it seems, a phenomenon only for the physical scientists.

DISCOVERY AS THE INCREMENTAL STEP; MOTIVATION AND COMMITMENT

Since Mrs. Eddy referred to Christian Science as a discovery, one who comes to make some commitment to the system she denominated Christian Science naturally asks if the word *discovery* is an apt one.

This is particularly so in light of the fact that she also referred to the purpose of Christian Science as restoring primitive Christianity, as a return to what had already existed during the first century.

A recent book called *Creativity: Genius and Other Myths* details the author's explanation of the creative process in a way that I find remarkably parallel to the experience of Mrs. Eddy. It, along with the discussion of scientific advances as being the establishment of new paradigms, goes a long way toward explaining the context in which Christian Scientists speak of Mrs. Eddy as discoverer.

The book's author, Robert Weisberg, takes the view that creativity is not the work of geniuses; it is society that later on attaches the label genius to someone for what he has created in either the sciences or the arts. It may also take away the label, as was the case with Johann Sebastian Bach for the century after his death, until his rediscovery by a new generation.[6]

Weisberg looks at the various psychological explanations of creativity and rather convincingly debunks them all: the role of the unconscious; sudden shafts of light that have no explainable source; the role of brainstorming, and divergent thinking. Rather, he makes a strong case that creativity is largely an incremental process. It is the result of a person adding something to what he already knows.

> . . . an incremental view of creativity leads to the expectation that even impressive creative products are rooted firmly in the experience of the creative individual and are developed gradually from his or her past work, and the work of others. Small steps, in this view, rather than great leaps, are the rule. Furthermore, the thought processes involved in great acts of creativity are like those found in more ordinary activities.[7]

This does not play down the role of the individual in discovering something new. In fact, the tenor of Weisberg's argument is entirely in line with Richard Bergland's assertion, quoted above, that new paths are generally charted by lone individuals.

But why does a particular individual happen to forge ahead? If it is not because he is a genius or has some particular grouping of talents that explains creativity, there must be some general explanation.

Weisberg finds it in two rather simple, related factors (in addition to his incremental view of creativity): the person's high level of motivation and his total absorption in his work.

> ... the creative genius is totally committed to work. The most influential scientists and artists in modern Western culture have had long careers characterized by very high productivity. Freud, for example, produced 330 publications in a forty-five-year career. Picasso produced several thousand works in seventy-five years; Einstein, 248 publications in fifty-three years, and Darwin, 119 in fifty-one years.[8]

Creative people are often so devoted to their work that they become virtually unaware of anything going on outside their own consciousness. This kind of absorption is one reason they succeed at what they are doing, since some discoveries happen only after many combinations of ideas have been tried. There is also a greater likelihood that deeply committed persons will make more of what may seem like chance occurrences that contribute to their discoveries, since the problems they are trying to solve are constantly on their minds.

This can be applied to virtually every person who contributed to the emancipation and growth of science in the post-Renaissance centuries. In looking at these people's discoveries with the instruments now available, much of what they discovered seems common sense. Yet for the most part they forged ahead on hunches that came out of long observation and cogitation over what the observations meant.

Until the time of Johannes Kepler, the astronomers were still trying to see the heavens through the mistaken belief of Ptolemy that the planets moved in circular orbit. Kepler, building on the astronomical sightings of Tycho Brahe, "tested *seventy* circular orbits against Tycho's Mars data, all to no avail. At one point ... he imagined himself on Mars, and sought to reconstruct the path the *earth's* motion would trace out across the skies of a Martian observatory; this effort consumed nine hundred pages of calculations, but still failed to solve the major problem." Finally, the answer hit him: the orbit of the planet is a perfect ellipse.[9] But this answer would not have come without the painstaking study of all the data he had available to him.

Just as notable was Sir Isaac Newton's work in establishing the first general laws of physics. Yet the same source as that about Kepler, Timothy Ferris, author of *Coming of Age in the Milky Way*, writes:

> Newton's surviving drafts of the *Principia* support Thomas Edison's dictum that genius is one percent inspiration and ninety-nine percent perspiration. Like Beethoven's drafts of the opening bars of the Fifth Symphony, they are characterized less by sudden flashes of insight than by a constant, indefatigable hammering away at immediate, specific problems; when Newton was asked years later how he had discovered his laws of celestial dynamics, he replied, "By thinking about them without ceasing." Toil was transmuted into both substance and veneer, and the finished manuscript, delivered to Halley in April 1686, had the grace and easy assurance of a work of art. For the modern reader the *Principia* shares with a few other masterworks of science—Euclid's *Elements* among them, and Darwin's *Origin of Species*—a kind of inevitability, as if its conclusions were self-evident. But the more we put ourselves into the mind-set of a seventeenth-century reader, the more it takes on the force of revelation. Never before in the history of empirical thought had so wide a range of natural phenomena been accounted for so precisely, and with such economy.[10]

✳ ✳ ✳

Creativity, by definition, also requires that there be a generally recognized important problem to be solved and that the solution be one that works. Now, applying that definition to the last half of Mary Baker Eddy's life, one can say that the problem was the age-old one, at least in Christianity: How could an all-powerful, all-good God create or tolerate the existence of evil? Her answer was unique, but it was grounded in the experience of Jesus. It was, in the words of Habakkuk: "God is of purer eyes than to behold evil."[11] The work of Jesus had shown that, to the godlike man, evil in all its forms had to be overcome and disappear. The answer, in other words, was not in philosophical reasoning but in demonstration. The answer was primarily in living form, as individual witness, which greatly limited one's ability to provide the answer only in writing. Similar to some of the modern theoretical physicists' assertions that reality is changed in the act of observation, God could not be an all-good, all-powerful God without man's active participation in the process, without his acceptance of God's good grace. Creation itself might then be seen as a continuously unfolding process, with new evidence each day of God's goodness, power, and loving control. God, we might say, requires man as the evidence of God's being and nature.

The next chapter will give somewhat more detail on Mrs. Eddy's own life. But to relate her to the Weisberg definition, she not only identified the problem to be solved but had the motivation to solve it. Her entire experience in a somewhat remote, rural New England area in the first half of the last century had been rooted in New England Calvinism. Its stern tenets strongly influenced her life from the time of girlhood. She grew up knowing that her life must be accountable to God. She was herself a semi-invalid almost her entire adult life until she began to see the mental nature of disease. During these years of limited activity she often bemoaned her inability to lead a full life or to do for others.

Her first experiences with the power of human thought to change conditions were with the attenuations of medicine she tried in homeopathy. Then she was temporarily helped by a well-known mesmerist. Although she outgrew the beliefs he worked with, or really became convinced that he had no firm idea of how he worked, her thought was being prepared to see the connection between mentality, the human consciousness, and the infinite consciousness that in religious terms she knew as God. She also had an accidental occurrence happen to her—literally, it was an accident to her body. And she later dated her discovery of Christian Science from the insight she had at the time of that accident. As soon as she had any awareness of the magnitude of what she had discovered, she felt impelled to begin sharing the discovery.

The incremental view of creativity does not negate the concept that an area of human knowledge occasionally needs a new paradigm. Christianity needed a new model. Seemingly hemmed in on all sides, first by the Newtonian revolution in physics, then by the acceptance of Darwin's evolution, and about to be inundated with theories about the role of the subconscious and unconscious or instinctual in what had seemed like a clockwork, consciously regulated mind, there seemed less and less important ground for traditional Christianity to stand on. All that seemed to remain was its emphasis on the highest ethical and moral code the world had yet seen—and there were many fine people who believed that such a code could be enforced without recourse to an ultimate cause.

For most of the twenty centuries following the life of Jesus, Christians had been unable to repeat the kind of demonstrations Jesus had routinely made. The *healing* Christ had been largely relegated by the theologians to the divinity that was unique to him in their theologies, instead of being a divinity that belongs to every man if he will only acknowledge and claim it. Without the proof that Jesus had provided of the existence of a spiritual law that could negate not only the practice of sin but also the experience of disease, Christianity no longer stood on the spiritual but also very practical level on which he had established it. Merely trying to live up to its ethical commands, as important as that was, did not bring the accompanying sense of rebirth that had exhilarated the first few generations of Christians.

In Mrs. Eddy's case, motivation and total commitment were present from the beginning. Her Christian background did not allow her to accept a healing only for herself. Pressed to find the explanation for what had happened to her, she proceeded to spend the rest of her life articulating the discovery, healing and teaching others how to heal, writing so that future generations could receive her message unadulterated, and setting up an institutional framework to promote her discovery after she was gone.

She clearly did not know in 1866 that she would still be at work in the year 1910. As long as ten years after the discovery, she still had no intention of starting a separate church denomination. Even after she had established a church in the 1880s, she talked and wrote frequently about finding others to carry on in her stead. But her own thinking on the Science she had founded was so far ahead of her students that almost by definition no such person or persons could emerge. (And those willing ones who did emerge had motives mixed with personal ambition.) For almost thirty years her correspondence refers to the fact that she had not had a vacation in—years (the number lengthening each year); after 1900 she seems to have realized that her work would keep her at her desk until the day she died. One can easily see how Weisberg's requirements of motivation and total commitment fit the life history of Mrs. Eddy. Whether she did solve the age-old problem of evil is something for each person to decide. That can be done only by going some part of the distance Mrs. Eddy walked and seeing if her way may indeed have been a replication for the twentieth and future centuries of the path Jesus laid out.

With this as background we now have the context for looking at the events leading up to Mrs. Eddy's discovery and at the discovery itself.

Chapter 6

THE NINETEENTH-CENTURY BACKGROUND

Before looking at the discovery of Christian Science itself, we need to consider the dominant elements in early nineteenth-century New England, where Mary Baker Eddy was raised. The most important, of course, had to be her own religious background, which was the rock-ribbed Puritanism that had flourished all over New England a century earlier and still held sway in the smaller towns such as her birthplace of Bow, New Hampshire. There had been more softening of the original Puritan doctrines in the larger cities of New England, and by the 1820s, Boston had been influenced by the "heresy" of Unitarianism.

The general optimism of the new republic also affected the mental atmosphere, as did the philosophy of transcendentalism, by which European romanticism and some Oriental thought entered America for the first time. Transcendentalism also had the effect of preparing the way in New England for the toleration of many diverse approaches to an individual's philosophy of life. To some extent, this made it easier for Christian Science to get a hearing when it burst upon the public's consciousness later in the century.

Finally, many pseudosciences, so-called, flourished during the nineteenth century. They were attempts to find either health or a more satisfying philosophy of life. Sometimes, as with mesmerism, they tried to be a combination of both. Mrs. Eddy herself was aware of several of these, and her knowledge of them at least indirectly served to center her own thinking on the possibility of there being a science behind the works of Jesus.

THE PURITAN LEGACY

The Puritans who came to New England were strongly motivated by a religious view of life. If ever there was a migration of people that can be seen as dominated by a religious vision, as opposed to one for economic or social reasons, this was it. Yet much about the Puritans is popularly misunderstood.

To begin with, in life-style the Puritans were the product of boisterous Elizabethan England. While trying to live a sober Christian life, they did not look or act entirely unlike their brethren back home. They did not dress in black and white (as the Quakers who came to Pennsylvania later were wont to do). When they could afford it, they enjoyed colorful clothes. Nor were they tee-totalers. They reveled in the common drinks of their day, and one of the early presidents of Harvard College was dismissed partly because of the allegedly inferior quality of the ale his wife produced for the students. Moreover, judging from the subjects of some of the sermons preached in the early days, it would seem that the Puritans indulged in about as much sexual misconduct as did their brothers back in England. In fact, if one will only think of them as Elizabethans, he will have a better understanding of the context of their daily living.

Perry Miller and Thomas Johnson, major intellectual historians of the Puritans, concluded: "There was nothing lukewarm, half-hearted, or flabby about the Puritan; whatever he did, he did with zest and gusto. In that sense we might say that though his life was full of anguish of spirit, he nevertheless enjoyed it hugely."[1]

The anguish of spirit arose, of course, from his religion. The Puritans were English Protestants who believed that the Church of England had not carried the Reformation far enough. Having broken with the pope over the Roman church's claim to final authority in religious matters, the Protestants looked to the Bible as their *sole* authority. The Puritans thought, however, that the English bishops were using the Bible as their authority only when it suited them, that there was an inconsistency in its application. They

> held that the Bible was sufficiently plain and explicit so that men with the proper learning, following the proper rules of deduction and interpretation, could establish its meaning and intention on every subject, not only in theology, but in ethics, costume, diplomacy, military tactics, inheritances, profits, marriages, and judicial procedure.[2]

The Puritans did not believe, on the other hand, that every man should interpret the Bible for himself. In the theocracy that they established in their first settlements in Massachusetts, the clergy were still the arbiters of orthodoxy. Those early settlers, such as Roger Williams, who insisted on the right of private interpretation, were driven out and became the founders of the neighboring colony of Rhode Island.

What was this theology for which the Puritans were willing to risk their lives in order to see it worked out in their new communities in New England? It was, in essence, the theology of Calvin, who had established his own theocracy in Geneva two generations earlier. For Calvin, God was essentially unknowable—the transcendent being of the Old Testament, as opposed to the more immanent sense of God made known through the life and works of Christ Jesus in the New Testament.

This does not quite mean that God was some kind of unknowable mystery hidden behind a thick black curtain. He was the almighty power depicted in the Old Testament who controlled the destinies of all mankind. But this all-powerful being was so different from what human beings could even imagine as to be indescribable. Puritanism "never forgot that at the long last God is not to be fathomed, understood or described with absolute certainty. . . . The essence of Calvinism and the essence of Puritanism is the hidden God, the unknowable, the unpredictable."[3]

Calvin "demanded that they contemplate, with steady, unblinking resolution, the absolute, incomprehensible, and transcendent sovereignty of God; he required men to stare fixedly and without relief into the very center of the blazing sun of glory."[4] Small wonder that the Puritan lived a life of severe anguish, if such a God was deciding his ultimate fate. One can even wonder, in this partial description of Calvinist Protestantism, how anyone gave up the comfort offered by his Catholic faith to become a Protestant.

But that was not the end of the story. It actually gets somewhat worse, and then it gets better. The "worse" part is the Calvinist theory of predestination. Stated very simply, this held that God already knows who will be "saved" and who will be damned. Just as the early church fathers had looked to Scripture for their authority, Calvin looked there also. And in the Epistle to the Romans, Paul's legalistic explanation of Christianity to the Romans, he found the verses (8:29, 30) suggesting that God had foreknowledge of those who would become the sons of God.

Now, if God already knows the outcome, of what use is it to try to live the moral demands of the Christian life? The English Calvinists, at least, worked their way around this dilemma through the development of what they called covenant theology. Without going into it any more deeply here, they worked out a scheme under which God was explained as having made a covenant with man to *try*, along with believing in Christ Jesus as his savior, to lead a moral life. Under this so-called covenant, Miller explains that

> if a man will believe, he will receive the grace enabling him to approximate a holy life, but his failure to reach perfection will not be held against him. . . . The regeneration of any man, as long as he is in the body, will be imperfect at best. It will manifest itself in a perpetual struggle to an unattainable end, and according to the covenant of grace God will accept the intention and the effort for the deed.[5]

Covenant theology made Calvinism tenable; it brought man back into his own salvation as an active agent, but an agent working with God's help. It combined Augustine's and Luther's theology of the grace of God with the motivation for man to strive continually to demonstrate, through his daily living, that he was among the elect. It accounts for the tension that was part of every Puritan's life. In its secularized version, which was more common in the larger metropolises of New England by Mrs. Eddy's day, it accounts for the belief that material prosperity itself was a sign of election, or of God's grace. If the process seemed convoluted by which Jesus' teachings became the theology of the Apostles' Creed some centuries later, the process by which some of the original Protestant dogma evolved during a period of great social and political change, as well as a changing cosmological outlook, has an equal number of twists and turns. Yet its original, pristine statement by the Puritan divines is what accounted for the tough fiber and serious moral outlook of the early Americans of New England.

One other factor needs to be explained and deserves to be honored: the Puritans' regard for education. The Puritans and the Anglicans disagreed on the use of reason as an aid in spiritual matters. The more urbane Anglicans saw reason as one faculty leading to truth, one of the ways, in fact, to understand the Bible. For the Puritan, however, without the regeneration of the human mind that comes through salvation, human reason would not begin to comprehend the message of the Bible.

> The Puritan is arguing that the source of truth is the Bible, read with the eye of grace, and therefore rationally understood. Reason does not prove the sense and intention of God . . . but the sense and intention of God instruct the reason. For the Puritan, reason does not make clear the sense of scripture, but the clear sense of scripture creates the reason.[6]

Mrs. Eddy speaks about the "unillumined human mind." She would have instinctively sided with the Puritans, being their spiritual heir, as it were. But the Puritans were not against learning. Mrs. Eddy would view the human intellect in a similar way. Her own theological upbringing undoubtedly made her aware that human intellect alone does not grasp spiritual truth, coming as it does from another dimension of consciousness. At the same time, her background gave her great respect for the abundant exercise of intellect, and her statement of Christian Science itself demands the exercise of a normal intellect to be sufficiently grasped.

Although the Puritan heritage in America split into many branches, the type of emotional, evangelistic fervor that periodically descends

on America even today was not part of the original heritage. (That
phenomenon, which is unique to America, is best explained by the
loneliness of the frontier and the need for emotional closeness that
some felt.) One should bear in mind, instead, the fact that only six
years after beginning the settlement in Boston, the Puritans established
a college a few miles west in Cambridge—a college for the training
of ministers.

> The greatness of the Puritans is not so much that they conquered
> a wilderness, or that they carried a religion into it, but that they
> carried a religion which, narrow and starved though it may have
> been in some respects, deficient in sensuous richness or brilliant
> color, was nevertheless indissolubly bound up with an ideal of
> culture and learning. In contrast to all other pioneers, they made
> no concessions to the forest, but in the midst of frontier con-
> ditions, . . . they maintained schools and a college, a standard of
> scholarship and of competent writing, a class of men devoted
> entirely to the life of the mind and of the soul.[7]

A religious frame of reference governed their lives. And it still governed the lives of men like Mark Baker and his family two hundred
years later. This is why no study of Christian Science can begin without an underlying appreciation of the biblical roots that lay behind
all the thoughts of Mary Baker Eddy, or her sense that nothing in life
had ultimate meaning except as it was connected to God. What Miller
and Johnson say of the Puritans applies equally to her: "[The
Puritan] lived in the world according to the principles that must gov-
ern this world, with an ever-present sense that they were only for the
time being and that his true home was elsewhere."[8]

Puritan thinking inevitably evolved in the nearly two centuries that
it dominated American religious life. The rise of rationalism in the
eighteenth century affected only a small proportion of the population, but many of the elite who wrote its founding documents (the
Declaration of Independence and later the U.S. Constitution) were
students of the Greek classics as well as of Locke and Rousseau. At
the time of the American Revolution, however, fully three-quarters
of the population of the colonies could be classified as Puritan in
belief. If those who came out of European continental countries

where their Protestantism had a direct line of descent from Calvin were added in, close to 90 percent of the new nation was of Puritan heritage. Either because of the reluctance of many intellectuals today to acknowledge America's religious past or because of their ignorance of this past, this heritage is not sufficiently taken into account in many of the books that attempt to explain the key elements in America's swift progress in its early years.

A NEW NATION AND ITS OPTIMISM; TRANSCENDENTALISM

If a latter-day Puritanism most nearly defines the mental climate in which Mrs. Eddy was raised, there were still other influences at work in her world. One general influence was the optimism of the new republic, and closely connected to this optimism was the warm, fuzzy philosophy of transcendentalism.

The optimism of the new country did not as easily extend itself to the hard-scrabble farming world of New Hampshire. But even there the literate population was aware of what was happening elsewhere. The new nation was just beginning to work out an intellectual independence to accompany the political freedom it had grown accustomed to even before the formal break with England.

As for transcendentalism, this philosophy never had any direct link with the discovery of Christian Science. It did, however, serve to further break down the rigidity of the religious atmosphere in New England. Many of the ideas that its leading philosopher, Ralph Waldo Emerson, promoted carried overtones reminiscent of the gnostics of the second century. They showed the readiness of thinking people to look again at the relationship of Christ Jesus to their contemporary lives.

* * *

The conditions of life in the new republic encouraged the individual to explore, to trample over the boundaries that another, older society would automatically have set for him. It was not a protective society, however, as most people have come to expect in the late twentieth century. If established institutions did not hinder an individual's own progress, neither were they a support on which to lean. Thus, the average man had of necessity a keen sense of responsibility for his and his family's development. And, at least for those who were not too burdened by the harshness of this responsibility, there also came the sense of new opportunity.

This helps explain why, when the essence of Christian Science came to Mrs. Eddy's thought in the 1860s, her lack of formal schooling or her noninvolvement with formal schools of theology would never have crossed her mind as a reason to doubt the validity of what she was seeing spiritually, or of her ability to carry forward her unique mission in life.

The previous chapter on the nature of discovery noted that motivation, inquisitiveness, the desire to get answers is always one part of the process. Why are things as they are? Are they really what they seem to be? and so on. At the time of America's bicentennial in 1976, a group of bicentennial scholars looking at America's past noted the work of an uneducated farmhand, Thomas Applegarth, who had been taught to read by a neighbor Quaker lady. (I am indebted to James Michener's novel *Chesapeake* for being aware of this example.)

Applegarth liked to study maps. He became fascinated with the shape of Chesapeake Bay and wondered how its waters had formed. Saving and borrowing some sixty dollars, he set off on his own expedition to find the headwaters of the Susquehanna River (it pours into the Chesapeake). The bicentennial scholars wrote:

> His general observations were extraordinary for his age. He seems to have anticipated theories far in advance of his time and to have foreseen quite accurately what later exploration would prove. [That part of his work] which has never been superseded was to view the Susquehanna riverine system, past and present, as an ecological whole. In his day this word had not been invented, but he invented the concept, and no team of contemporary engineers and environmentalists has ever had a clearer picture of the Susquehanna and its interrelationships. He has been an inspiration to generations of American scientists, and no one who has followed his sixty-dollar exploration to that final day when he stood at the veritable headwaters of the Susquehanna can forget

his description of that moment: "I stood in that meadow with the sun reflecting back from the isolated drops of water and realized that for a river like the Susquehanna there could be no beginning. It was simply there, the indefinable river, now broad, now narrow, in this age turbulent, in that asleep, becoming a formidable stream and then a spacious bay and then the ocean itself, an unbroken chain with all parts so interrelated that it will exist forever, even during the next age of ice."[9]

While the discovery Mrs. Eddy was to announce to the world was of an entirely different nature, Thomas Applegarth's story indicates something of the kind of pioneering quality that was part of the air of nineteenth-century America.

* * *

At the same time that Mary Baker was a child in New Hampshire, the Congregational church in New England had gone through the throes of the Unitarian controversy. Unitarianism, which has never been strong in terms of numbers in the United States, had become the "other" church in much of New England (besides the Congregational church, descended from the Puritans). It was introduced into America from England, although its origins were in the heart of the European continent. From the early days of the Reformation, there had been small splinter groups on the continent who broke with the doctrine of the Trinity and the divinity of Jesus. Breaking with the orthodox doctrine of the divinity of Christ Jesus, the denomination also became a haven for rationalist thinkers who still wished to maintain a foot in their ancestral Christian home.

The denomination is mentioned at this point solely because it preceded the development of transcendentalism. Transcendentalism's most famous philosopher, Emerson, was himself a former Unitarian minister. Many of his broadsides aimed at the organized church were directed most particularly against the rationalist Unitarian church he had known in Massachusetts.

Transcendentalism itself arose out of the migration to America of some of the Romantic movement in Europe; it also included America's first brush with Oriental thought. The writers and thinkers who called themselves transcendentalists were too loose a band and too disorganized in thought to be taken seriously as full-fledged philosophers. Moreover, in the rush of events that was to follow—the antislavery emotions of the 1840s and 1850s, the Civil War, the completion of the westward movement after the Civil War, and the rapid industrialization of the eastern half of the nation—transcendentalism can be made to look like a puny sideshow alongside the colorful circus tent of boisterous late nineteenth-century America.

Yet it was an important catalyst. Octavius B. Frothingham, himself a Unitarian clergyman, wrote the standard history of transcendentalism in the 1870s. Noting that it had "but one generation of births," he concluded, perhaps only a bit generously:

> Transcendentalism was an episode in the intellectual life of New England; an enthusiasm, a wave of sentiment, a breath of mind that caught up such as were prepared to receive it, elated them, transported them, and passed on,—no man knowing whither it went. Its influence on thought and life was immediate and powerful. Religion felt it, literature, laws, institutions. To the social agitations of forty years ago it was invaluable as an inspiration. The various reforms owed everything to it. New England character received from it an impetus that never will be spent.[10]

It is not unjust to the movement to take Emerson as its most representative spokesman. Trained as a minister at Harvard, he came closest to expressing the transcendentalists' views as a philosophy and was also a master of nineteenth-century essay style. His life of intellectual and spiritual speculation, as expressed in his books of essays, still has much that could engage the widening horizons of high school and college students today.

It was his essays and, in particular, two speeches he made at Harvard that expressed the ideas for which he and the transcendentalists are remembered. His Phi Beta Kappa address in 1836 was widely recognized as America's declaration of intellectual independence from Europe. On the other hand, his address to the graduating class of the Divinity School so scandalized Harvard that he was not invited back for another speech for almost thirty years.

Emerson said in a variety of intriguing ways that man is responsible for his own salvation. Yet he did not weave his beliefs into a metaphysical tapestry that others might use. There is little in his writing that makes one believe he knew how to deal with the depths of evil in human thought. There is instead, in Emerson, as in most of the transcendentalist thought, the feeling of a warm spring afternoon when all the earth is bursting forth with new life. Enjoy! (as the waiters in restaurants say today) it seems to say. Whether this suffices for dealing with the cold of a January night is another matter. Yet, if his philosophy misses the hard demands of genuine Christianity, one can still appreciate his reminder that each of us has his own destiny to work out.[11]

In an essay called "The Over-Soul" (a word that came close to his definition of God), Emerson wrote:

> All goes to show that the soul in man is not an organ, but animates and exercises all the organs; is not a function, like the power of memory, of calculation, of comparison, but uses these as hands and feet; is not a faculty, but a light; is not the intellect or the will, but the master of the intellect and the will; is the background of our being, in which they live,—an immensity not possessed and that cannot be possessed.

As for man, he said that what we commonly call man, "the eating, drinking, planting, counting man, does not, as we know him, represent himself, but misrepresents himself." He was not far from the metaphysical stand Mrs. Eddy would later take that mortal man is a misrepresentation of the real man.

He had an appreciation for the role of revelation, although somewhat like the gnostics he believed that no revelation could ever be final. "We distinguish the announcements of the soul, its manifestations of its own nature, by the term Revelation. These are always attended by the emotion of the sublime. For this communication is an influx of the Divine mind into our mind."

Yet, if man wanted to hear what God had to reveal to him, "he must 'go into his closet and shut the door,' as Jesus said. God will not make himself manifest to cowards. He must greatly listen to himself, withdrawing himself from all the accents on other men's devotion."

Emerson carried this accent on each person's individual responsibility even further in "Self-Reliance," where he wrote:

> The objection to conforming to usages that have become dead to you is that it scatters your force. It loses your time and blurs the impression of your character. If you maintain a dead church, contribute to a dead Bible-society, vote with a great party either for the government or against it, spread your table with base housekeepers,—under all these screens I have difficulty to detect the precise man you are: and of course so much force is withdrawn from your proper life. But do your work, and I shall know you. Do your work, and you shall reinforce yourself.

Although Emerson could not deviate from his emphasis on the individual's own responsibility for his salvation, he saw Jesus as an illustrious example. In the Divinity School address, for example, he said:

> . . . the unique impression of Jesus upon mankind, whose name is not so much written as ploughed into the history of this world, is proof of the subtle virtue of this infusion. . . . Jesus Christ belonged to the true race of prophets. He saw with open eye the mystery of the soul. Drawn by its severe harmony, ravished with its beauty, he lived in it, and had his being there. Alone in all history he estimated the greatness of man. One man was true to what is in you and me. He saw that God incarnates himself in man, and evermore goes forth anew to take possession of his World.

It was the "noxious exaggeration about the person of Jesus" that angered Emerson. "In how many churches, by how many prophets, tell me, is man made sensible that he is an infinite Soul; that the earth and heavens are passing into his mind; that he is drinking forever the soul of God?" It was beginning to indicate some strength of character, he said, "to withdraw from the religious meetings."

For all his effusiveness over the immanence of God in man, he had no instruction in how to experience it. He appreciated Jesus but did not see that Jesus' unique role in history was more than *an* example. However, somewhat prophetically, he did say:

> It is the office of a true teacher to show us that God is, not was;
> that He speaketh, not spake. The true Christianity,—a faith like
> Christ's in the infinitude of man,—is lost. . . . I look for the new
> Teacher that shall follow so far those shining laws that he shall
> see them come full circle.

Emerson did not foresee that the new teacher might be a woman
and that her writings would indeed come "full circle." Yet he himself came close, in his emphasis on the individual's own responsibility,
to defining the style of the "new" Christianity that was less than a
generation from being articulated in his own New England.

Emerson's transcendentalism can be described as a kind of "soft metaphysics." It laid the responsibility on the individual to find his own meaning in life but lacked any integrated guidance for the search. It
suggested the reality of a perfect universe beyond the material senses'
cognition but failed to make any attempt to deal with the contradictory
evidence of imperfection and evil presented by these same senses.

By denying the uniqueness, the eschatology, of historical Christianity,
the transcendentalists ultimately were a factor in the weakening of the
moral and ethical mold of orthodox Christianity, which had contributed
so enormously to the intellectual and moral fiber of early America. On
the positive side, however, by loosening thought from its orthodox
moorings, transcendentalism did help to make the mental climate of
New England somewhat more receptive for the claims of a scientific
Christianity that Mrs. Eddy would shortly be making.

PANACEAS AND PSEUDOSCIENCES

Transcendentalism might be described as a secular religion—but one
without a church, since every transcendentalist would be harking to
his own inner voice.

We turn now to discuss a few of the nineteenth-century movements
that could not even be called secular religion. They did, however, have
certain religious connotations. And, for some people who followed them,
they offered some of the comfort usually associated with religion.
Among the panaceas and pseudosciences of that century were, most particularly, hydropathy, homeopathy, mesmerism, and spiritualism.

Hydropathy

Hydropathy and homeopathy were solely medical fads. Hydropathy, or the water cure, had been started by a German farmer in Silesia in the 1820s. Within a decade or slightly more it had spread to England. In 1842 a hydropathic institute was founded in London, and the spas at Bath were done over to follow the rules of the German founder, Vincent Priessnitz.[12]

Hydropathy soon found a fertile field in the United States, where the era of the common man, ushered in by Andrew Jackson, was one in which people were ripe for criticizing established, "elite" author-ity—in this case, the authority of the regular medical profession. "It is little wonder that Americans, observing the debilitating effects that eclectic physicians had on patients, would seek cures that promised less shock to the body and seemed, at least initially, just as effective in their curative powers."[13]

There was, incidentally, often much more to the cure than just drinking waters at the spas. Hydropathy also involved the use of cold wet sheets and hot wool blankets. Yet it was not only (or even par-ticularly) the uneducated who followed the system. In England, Alfred, Lord Tennyson wrote, "Much poison has come out of me, which no physic ever would have brought to light."[14]

The movement peaked by the 1850s. Mrs. Eddy herself had a brief experience at a hydropathic institute before meeting the mesmerist Phineas Quimby, who would act as a much larger catalyst on the development of her thought. That something like the water cure could achieve as much public esteem as it did is a measure not only of human gullibility but also of the low estate that established medical practice had among some of the public. By the end of the century orthodox medicine would be well on its way to establishing itself—and being accepted—as a scientific practice, while fifty years earlier it was competing not only with cures such as hydropathy but, more important, with homeopathy.

Homeopathy

Homeopathy, according to one expert on the subject, "repre-sented the last of the major systems to flourish before the onrush of extensive advance in germ theory, treatment of infection, pathology, and pharmaco-therapeutics."[15] It alleged to use minute quantities of a drug that, if given to a healthy person, would result in symptoms like those of the person who was ill. The drug was so attenuated that the question came to be whether the drug had any effect at all, or whether it was the belief of the patient in the entire process that governed the outcome.

As bizarre as its description may sound to ears today, an entire branch of medicine was built up around homeopathy following the leading of a German doctor, Samuel Hahnemann. It arrived in the United States about 1825. As with hydropathy, interest in it was among all classes. The American poet William Cullen Bryant tried homeopathy for himself. Washington Irving, another early American author, was ill a good part of his life and first learned of homeopathy when traveling in Europe in the 1820s. He turned to it as his main means of medicine, and was being treated by a homeopathic doctor when he died in 1859.[16]

Nor were these the only cure-alls. Some of the pseudosciences allegedly had a social purpose. Phrenology, for instance, which claimed to measure both intellect and moral proclivities by the shape of the skull, also had as its goal moral reforms. The proliferation of so many new systems of thought based on some false premise may seem like an object lesson in the laziness of the human mind, as a result of which masses of people can be led to accept new claims because they offer an easy way out of some problem. On the other hand, these pseudosciences also indicate the kind of searching for solutions and willingness to question established authority that was ongoing in nineteenth-century America. (This was not happening just in the United States; however, in the older societies of Western Europe there was, in general, a more settled, sober mentality and the need for social acceptance on a larger scale than prevailed in America.)

Spiritualism

Two other pseudoscientific movements tell even more about the mind of America in the mid-nineteenth century: spiritualism and mesmerism. Unfortunately for Americans, no European country can be listed as spiritualism's place of origin. Its most flagrant expression, in the form of seances, mediums, and rappings, dates back to the Fox sisters in New York State. However, it survived for several decades as an important movement because of the work of Andrew Jackson Davis, whose dates (1826–1910) are almost identical with those of Mrs. Eddy.

Davis was aware of the millennial movements afoot in the United States of his youth. He had also heard of the Swedish theologian Emanuel Swedenborg, whose work had influenced many thinkers in nineteenth-century New England. And he was acquainted with hypnotism. "The discovery of a new science by which communication with the dead could be achieved did not seem improbable to many optimistic Americans who viewed innovative technical inventions and listened to lecturers extol the limitless horizon of the human mind," writes Robert W. Delp in an essay on spiritualism.[17]

Davis developed a "harmonial philosophy" by which he hoped to reform the "existing social, economic, and religious systems." The ideas by which he proposed doing this were supposed to have come to him from spirits in another world. Between the writings of Davis and the "rappings" of the Fox sisters, spiritualism came to interest perhaps as many as a million people in the northeastern United States. The spiritualists also hoped to use their movement to spearhead social reform. In New York City, they supported the Children's Progressive Lyceum and the Moral Police Fraternity, both organizations designed to deal with the growing social problems of New York.

Davis went on to get a medical degree later in his career, and spoke vaguely as if he recognized the mental causation of disease. He said, for instance, that "every cutaneous disease, every tumor, every disorganization in the substance or appendages or organs is in effect disturbed and diseased psychical or spiritual force."[18]

Yet Davis himself had no use for organized religion. Like Quimby, the mesmerist with whom Mrs. Eddy was to get acquainted, Davis did talk about a Christ-principle. His harmonial philosophy, however, did not acknowledge the historical role of Jesus as either personal savior or exemplar, nor did he discuss the need for human redemption in Christian terms.

We can identify in both spiritualism and mesmerism the process by which the public's thought at large was being loosed from a biblical basis and turned toward what would become an immense interest in psychology in the twentieth century. Davis himself claimed to be a medium.

> He believed, however, that true spiritualism implied a great deal more than contacting or communing with those who had once lived on earth. Instead, it was a means of illuminating the darkness of earth with the light of distant realms even then moving earth toward the dawn of a new and brighter day.[19]

It may seem strange that this help, which it was acknowledged had to come from outside the normal commonsense realm of material life, had to be described in the language of spiritualism. Why, one might ask, could it not have been identified with the salvation that comes through Christ, with the acknowledgment of God's law and its operation in the affairs of humankind just as in the life of Christ Jesus?

The answer seems to be that the Bible, in spite of three hundred years of Protestantism, was not yet an open book but only a book with many and confusing interpretations. These interpretations, whether based on a literal or a metaphorical reading of the Bible, had less and less relevance in an age impressed by tangible scientific accomplishments, the basis of which seemed to confront and contradict the Bible.

Delp summarizes the life of Andrew Jackson Davis:

> In that experimental period of change, transition, and boundless hope, Davis reflected the basic American millenarian tradition. Excited by the Millerite enthusiasm of 1843, he delivered his Revelations somewhat later, when Fourierism and Swedenborgianism preserved the same dream of a new heaven and a new earth. Davis also shared a not uncommon belief that the New World provided an appropriate setting for the millennium.[20]

There is absolutely no connection between the theory behind spiritualism and Christian Science. However, Mrs. Eddy frequently had to defend herself from the charge, sometimes maliciously made, that she either believed in spiritualism or was a medium herself. Some of her very early students had had connections with spiritualism. But it was their lack of ties with organized orthodoxy that made them flexible enough to listen to Mrs. Eddy's teachings, not any similarity between those teachings and spiritualism.

Mesmerism

So we come to mesmerism, or hypnotism, the last of the pseudoscientific cults to flourish in the nineteenth century. One may say that hypnotism is not only a nineteenth-century cult, but that it is even a partially respectable medical tool today. That is correct. But its use is more limited. One may make a comparison with hydropathy. The presence of indoor pools, health spas, and saunas has some relation to the hydropathic craze of the last century, but their proponents avoid the panacealike claims that hydropaths made. Likewise, the hypnotism of today avoids the extravagant claims made for it in the late eighteenth and nineteenth centuries and concentrates instead on the relieving of pain or on some kind of mental recall under a psychotherapist's care.

Hypnotism got its start from the work of a Viennese doctor, Anton Mesmer, in the 1770s. Mesmer believed he had discovered a bodily fluid that responded to magnetism—hence the original phrase, animal magnetism. It was allegedly dislocations in this fluid that caused many diseases. Although the fluid proved quite as ephemeral as the alchemists' phlogiston or the physicists' theory of the ether, Mesmer attracted a wide following among the rich in prerevolutionary France.

Mesmer eventually discovered that he could often have the same effect on a patient by merely passing his hand over the patient's body, without the use of a magnet. This might have been proof enough that there was no such thing as animal magnetism. But from this evolved the concept of one person's having influence on the health or thoughts of another. The concept of animal magnetism itself was thoroughly looked into in 1784 by a royal commission, of which Benjamin Franklin, as the first American ambassador to France and one of the world's leading scientists at the time, was a member. The commission did a remarkably thorough, objective study of patients in as tightly controlled a situation as possible. Its conclusion was that animal magnetism was a hoax.

Mesmerism lived on, not because of its discoverer's original mistake, but because the mesmerists learned the power of hypnotism. One of Mesmer's most brilliant students, the Marquis de Puysegur, learned to put his patients into a trance. In this state, they often spoke above the level of either their personal education or their social standing. And a few of them even became clairvoyant or telepathic while under hypnosis. This discovery, that there was a significant stratum of mental life going on beneath the surface of consciousness, was to lead in the next century to many of the techniques used by psychiatry today in its attempt to uncover an individual's total personality.

A student of de Puysegur's, another Frenchman by the name of Poyen, came on a lecture tour to New England. His interest in mesmerism was more in its ability to explore (and exploit) the areas of consciousness below those normally experienced than in healing illness. He also found that a small percentage of those whom he hypnotized manifested clairvoyance or telepathy while under his influence. By the 1840s there were some two hundred mesmerists practicing in Boston alone.

Spiritualism had attracted some followers because of its implied guarantee of a life after death. After all, if there could be even one-way communication with the dead, there must be more to life than the senses here on earth could understand. Mesmerism satisfied a spiritual lack in another area. In even partially proving a link between body and mind, or between the minds of two persons, it seemed to prove the existence of a kind of spiritual unity that is one of the elements most of mankind yearns for. People who became involved in it, or at least some of them, believed "that the mesmerizing process helped them to reestablish inner harmony with the very source of physical and emotional well-being. While in the mesmeric state, they learned that disease and even moral confusion were but the unfortunate consequences of having fallen out of rapport with the invisible spiritual workings of the universe."[21]

For the traditional Christian, whatever experience the person under hypnosis had was certainly not "spiritual." On the other hand, hypnotism did serve to show that there is more to experience than meets the eye—the five physical senses, that is.

Robert C. Fuller, writing the essay on mesmerism in the book *Pseudo Science and Society in 19th-Century America*, takes a more positive view of mesmerism's contribution to American life than might someone who was especially concerned about the potential evil effects of mesmerism in terms of one person's yielding his mentality even temporarily to the control of another. But Fuller's comments serve to place mesmerism in the context of its contribution to the lives of those who were fascinated by it at the time:

> Its psychological terminology transposed the form of personal piety from categories of theological transcendence to those of psychological immanence, thus accommodating the conceptual needs of an increasingly pluralistic culture. [It was the first of many successive psychological systems that have] attracted popular followings precisely because large segments of the American public are continuously seeking ways to reduce their metaphysical responsibilities to more manageable proportions.[22]

And that statement is a fitting denouement to the history of at least part of American culture from the landing of the Pilgrims to the middle of the nineteenth century. From a band of sturdy pioneers looking straight into the eye of a God they feared to a restless, opportunistic people rushing to get ahead in this land of opportunity but with "reduced metaphysical responsibilities"! Some of them, or maybe even most of them. But not all of them. From this brief review of some of the dominant themes in American life—

- the remnant of Calvinism, which focused Mrs. Eddy's own experience on the traditional God of the Bible;
- the optimism and expansive character of the new republic, which gave men and women in America an opportunity to work out the ideals of the Enlightenment in a more open-ended manner than was then possible in the older societies of Europe;
- the opening of religious thought that occurred from the influence of transcendentalism on American intellectual life in general; and

- the flowering of the various pseudosciences in an age that was turning to the relation of cause and effect in all areas of life, hoping to break through the mental and physical chains that still prevented many people from living up to the potential of their human lives—

we turn now to look at the life of a woman whose experience in some ways reflects the influence of all these elements.

MARY BAKER EDDY; THE DISCOVERY

This is not the book to relate in detail the life story of the discoverer of Christian Science, Mary Baker Eddy. Rather, this is primarily an effort to locate Christian Science as being at the center of the two-millennia-old attempt to tell once more the story of Jesus—the meaning of his life and works.

Yet this system of thought did come as a discovery to Mrs. Eddy, and now that we have looked briefly at some of the general mental forces at work in her nineteenth-century world, as well as at some current theories on the nature of discovery, this is an appropriate place to tell briefly how Christian Science entered Mrs. Eddy's life. For "enter" it did. She at no time had any notion that she was beginning something of her own invention.

Mrs. Eddy was a product of the later stages of old-style Calvinism. Growing up as the youngest of six children on a New Hampshire farm (she was born in 1821), she was used to hearing theology discussed around the family fireplace. The parish minister was a friend of the family's and would frequently come calling. Her own parents represented the two opposite faces of orthodox Congregational Christianity of her day, her father being the old-style ramrod Calvinist and her mother a warm, gentle, loving woman.

Mrs. Eddy, born Mary Baker, was a delicate child herself. Marrying at the age of twenty-two and moving south with her husband, she was widowed in less than a year and came home to deliver the child she was carrying. Not strong enough to care for him after his birth, she spent close to ten years living first with her parents, then with her widowed father until he remarried. She was a semi-invalid during much of this period. She seems to have had some kind of spinal difficulty for years. She was also keenly sensitive to the thoughts of others, and one can picture the displacement this young, but fast becoming middle-aged woman in nineteenth-century America must have felt. She felt she had talent to do many things, and occasionally wrote for local periodicals. But to her family she was just a young (and semi-invalided) widow, the kind of burden large families were used to putting up with.

She was rescued briefly from the humdrum of this existence by marriage to an itinerant dentist in 1853. She said later that she married him because he promised to provide a home for her son. But soon after this second marriage, to Dr. Patterson, the family that had been raising her son moved to the Dakotas—with him. She lost track of the son until sometime after the Civil War. Her own health continued to be a problem, and the good dentist frequently left her alone as he went his rounds in the state of New Hampshire.

About 1860 Mrs. Patterson heard of some healing work being done by a magnetic healer, Dr. Phineas P. Quimby, up in Portland, Maine. In the meantime she had been studying and even doing some of her own experimenting with homeopathy, which was a serious rival to "normal" medicine, as the last section showed. Getting no help from that quarter for her own illnesses, however, she became interested in what Dr. Quimby might be able to do for her. Her oldest sister, who had some responsibility for her and also was a well-to-do woman by this time, tried to prevent her from going to Quimby. But eventually, in 1862, Mrs. Eddy did manage to make her own arrangements to get to Portland. Within a few days of meeting Quimby, she was climbing the steps to the highest tower in Portland and appeared to be healed.

Then followed four years of mental development, which we are still able to follow only in part. Convinced that Quimby was not only the answer to her prayers for health but the answer for others also, she tried to find out what method he had used to heal her. His practice consisted of some mild forms of physical manipulation, such as the laying on of hands, and his patients (mostly women) had to wet their hair before their sessions with him. He did not practice outright hypnotism; yet he had begun his own trade as a hypnotist. Along with whatever manipulation was involved in his treatment, he certainly tried to make some kind of diagnosis of the condition and direct the patient's thought. In this sense he was a mesmerist. He also practiced by what came to be called absent treatment—that is, by thinking about or directing his mental thought-forces toward a person who was not physically present—and there exist several letters in which Mrs. Patterson wrote him to "come to her" at a certain hour, meaning to think about her condition at that particular time.[23]

In later years, when Christian Science had become a major presence on the Boston scene, one of Quimby's other patients, Julius Dresser, claimed that Mrs. Eddy had stolen all she knew from Quimby. This is patently untrue, and no one reading what became known as the Quimby manuscripts can find much resemblance in their overall structure with the thought of Christian Science. Where Mrs. Eddy came to posit a wholly spiritual universe and a metaphysics that is derived wholly from her definition of a spiritual God, the God of both the Old Testament and the New, Quimby's writings contain a confusing mixture of pseudoscience about how the mesmerist can supposedly work to make bodily fluids function differently, and so on, along with some discussion of Jesus that does recognize the distinction between Jesus and the Christ.

One difficulty in dealing with the Quimby papers is that, because of the argument that arose about Mrs. Eddy's own discovery, the Quimby family became reluctant to share the doctor's papers. During the years of the Dresser controversy, which was kept alive until about 1900, the papers continued to be withheld. When they were finally given to the Library of Congress in 1921, they were given with the unusual stipulation that the original papers could never be examined. To this day those visiting the Library of Congress and wishing to see the papers can only see copies.

One possible explanation of this (and there may be others) is that, although the documents are genuine, they may have been back-dated by Phineas Quimby's son. What would have been the purpose? One purpose could have been to make it appear that his father had had some of the ideas that actually came first to Mrs. Eddy. In any case, even if that is so, the ideas were not fully formed. Nor do the religious references appear to be those of a man of genuine spirituality. For Quimby also wrote that he had no interest in the morals of a man, that they made no difference in his ability to heal him.[24] For Mrs. Eddy, on the other hand, the connection of sin with sickness was as obvious as it was to the early church fathers.

What is of lasting importance is that Mrs. Eddy did not stay healed by Quimby. She was lifted out of her semi-invalid state, but she had various bouts with illness that did not respond to his treatment as well as she had at first. So she came to question whether he had a secure method of healing, one that could be transmitted to others. During this period, however, she had several lengthy sessions with Quimby. These occurred in 1862 and 1864. She said later that they shared their jottings, and some of the things that later appeared in his manuscripts may have been some of Mrs. Eddy's early, half-formed ideas about a Science of Christianity based on Jesus' life and works. For while she was becoming familiar with the workings of mesmerism, she had also retained her lifelong interest in evangelical Christianity. During the long years in the 1850s, when she was alone much of the time, she had continued to study her Bible and to question why a life such as hers should appear so useless in light of the kind of useful, abundant living Jesus' mission, including his healing work, had seemed to make available for mankind.

On January 15, 1866, Quimby died. Two weeks later Mrs. Eddy was seriously injured in a fall on some ice in the town where she was then living—Swampscott, Massachusetts. She wrote later that the doctor in charge had held out no hope for her recovery; at the very least, there was agreement all around that her injuries were extremely severe. Then, on the following Sunday morning, three days after the fall, not willing to accept the doctor's verdict, she lay in bed pondering the ninth chapter of Matthew. This happens to be the same chapter of the Bible that Clement of Alexandria had used as a text to show the connection of the healing of sin and sickness by Jesus (a coincidence surely unknown to her!). As she thought about that healing, she suddenly found herself healed, and got out of bed and walked.

This healing was not as complete at the time as the drama of that particular day would indicate. A few days later she wrote to Julius

Dresser, the Quimby patient she knew, asking him to help her. Dresser replied that he didn't know how to help his own wife.[25] So Mrs. Eddy realized at this moment that she was alone to ferret out the meaning of what she had briefly seen the morning she healed herself.

That is the simple beginning of Christian Science. For the next few years, Mrs. Eddy lived almost as an itinerant. Her sister refused to continue supporting her if she followed this new notion of hers. Her husband, Patterson, had come home briefly after being interned for a while in the Civil War. But the "discovery" had put her life on a new path, and she instinctively knew she had to fight it out alone. His own itinerant practice had also encouraged some errant social habits, and she quietly divorced him on grounds of adultery a few years later.

The purpose of this essay is to introduce Christian Science as a part, perhaps the final part, of the Christian spectrum that has flowed for two thousand years from the time of Jesus. So there is not adequate space here to interrupt the flow of metaphysical and religious development with the details of Mrs. Eddy's own personal development. That is the subject of several biographies already.

There does, however, need to be a brief discussion of the steps Mrs. Eddy took in the succeeding years. One looks at her as the lonely, ill, middle-aged woman she was before 1862. One looks at her again as she was in 1867 and 1868, years of extreme hardship in which she sometimes literally did not know where she would spend the next night, but years in which she was following an inner light to a known destination. And one looks at her again around the turn of the century, a woman of eighty by then. She had become the leader of what was becoming a worldwide religious movement. She was besieged with the problems any movement might have that challenged both the medical and the ecclesiastical hierarchies of her day and was being built with people who themselves had varying degrees of understanding of Christian Science. Yet she had become spiritually poised, alert to the dangers about her, and ready to handle whatever challenges remained (and several did remain) during the last ten years of her life. There are few stories to equal the change and growth that occurred in Mrs. Eddy herself between the ages of forty-five and ninety.

What is of most interest is simply the outline of steps she took following 1866. Mrs. Eddy came to Christian Science not from a deep, academic kind of study of the Bible or of Christian theology. But she did know her Bible and she did have a thorough grounding in the kind of Protestant theology that had culminated in New England Calvinism. This Calvinism in one sense remained the bedrock of her theology, in its undeviating looking to God as the source from which everything flows. In another sense, Christian Science was a contradiction of her Calvinist background, since she could not believe that the absolute God she had grown to trust could have created the material universe or the contradictions inherent in such a view of reality. She knew she had had a vision of another kind of reality but was unsure of its exact outline. For the next three years, she healed patients who came to her and continued studying her Bible.

She gradually realized that she had, as it were, backed into Christian Science. If one thinks of Science as the explanation of how Jesus worked, how he prayed, how he communed with the infinite intelligence Mrs. Eddy equated with God, then mesmerism and hypnotic suggestion could readily be understood as the extremes of a false kind of mental practice, a practice based on the belief that the human mind itself can control people and events. (And the "unextreme" or normal kind of mental activity could be seen as the undisciplined activity of the human mind, sometimes yielding to false, mesmeric suggestion, sometimes reacting to the intimations of a higher consciousness that are present in every human being.) One way of describing the situation is to say that in this nineteenth-century America, experimenting with other pseudosciences, the mesmeric practice of Quimby was one form of pseudoscience mimicking the about-to-be-discovered real science of Christianity. There is an irony here, in that without Christian Science Quimby would be a footnote, if that, in books about nineteenth-century America. However, his role in Mrs. Eddy's own development is that of a catalyst—in chemistry, an element without which two or more other elements cannot have the desired chemical reaction. The Quimby experience helped to prepare her thought to glimpse what she eventually did about the entirely spiritual practice of Christianity. At the very least, she needed some similar experience to illustrate for her that the working of the human mind, of human will, of one person's trying to influence another, was entirely separate in nature from an individual's becoming aware of the will of God.

Through her experience with Quimby, as well as some bad experiences on the part of some of her early students, she saw the dangers of mental control by an unchristly thought. She also saw, as in her healing from the effects of her fall on the ice, the quick results that could come from a simple yielding to the thought that God is present and in control through the operation of his eternal spiritual laws.

After she had shown that she could systematically heal, that her method of praying was indeed efficacious, she took the next step. She had to see if she could teach others the system she had discovered. If not, her discovery would die with her. So, starting in 1870, she began to teach Christian Science in Lynn, Massachusetts. This was a factory town, and her early students were not from Harvard College. Not that intellect alone would have made anyone a Christian Scientist. But she attracted those who were curious; some couldn't understand her; some eventually turned against her and tried to use what little they had learned to hurt her; and a few put it all to good, unselfish use. Satisfied that she could impart this knowledge to at least some fraction of those who heard her, she realized that the main way to perpetuate the teaching would have to come from writing. So, from 1872 to 1874, she interrupted almost all her other work to write a textbook. With much difficulty, she managed to bring out the book at her own expense in 1875 under the title *Science and Health*.

The year 1875 did not mean the end of all her trials. Those she would have in one form or another until her work was finished, and that was not to be until 1910. But 1875 marks a watershed in the history of Christian Science. With the textbook in print, the future of Christian Science did not rest entirely on Mrs. Eddy's personality or presence. She became Mary Baker Eddy, incidentally, on New Year's Day 1877, when she married a student, Asa Gilbert Eddy, who helped her in her work for the next five years until his passing in 1882. She was fifty-five years old when she married Eddy. There is no doubt that they shared a genuine emotional bond, but Eddy as her husband also freed her during those early years to concentrate on her work by removing would-be suitors whose motives in getting close to Mrs. Eddy might be mixed. Before she passed on, she was to have more than one encounter with persons who wanted to wrest control of the growing movement from her.

She moved to Boston in 1882 and remained there until 1889. During these years, she frequently preached to her growing church in public halls or temples belonging to other denominations. The 1880s were years in which Christian Science began to take on national dimensions. These were years in which Mrs. Eddy continued teaching and placing students in various fields where they themselves would both heal and teach. And she continued to work at her writings.

The textbook itself went through several major revisions, the most important being in 1891 and again in 1902. She kept it at her bedside and continued to look for the most exact way to state the science that she felt had been revealed to her. However, the major breakthrough that Christian Science represents in both theology and practice is already there in that first 1875 edition. Although her written presentation of it improved over the years, there are also major portions of the book that have changed very little from her earliest articulation of Christian Science in that first edition.

In 1889 Mrs. Eddy left Boston quite suddenly. It is still not entirely clear what motivated the move. It was partly that the demands on her for teaching were increasing more than her ability to meet them. She was close to seventy years of age, which in the nineteenth century must have seemed older than it does to us today. Moreover, she had undertaken a heroic work in what was still a man's world, and had to shoulder a kind of criticism that would not have come her way had she been born a man. The tone of the invective sometimes directed at her by conservative clergymen had a sexist vitriol connected to it.

In retrospect, her life in Boston seems to have been completed by 1889. She had taught about seven hundred students during those years, and the Christian Science movement had sufficient seedlings in it to begin to sprout on its own. She wanted to make a major revision of her textbook, and she proceeded to do that as soon as she was settled in New Hampshire.

More important, though, she had organizational changes to think through. Just as the full import of what she had to teach did not dawn on her all at once in 1866, she had come step by step to see that what amounted to a radical new form of Christian practice had to be protected for some time to come if it was to survive her own lifetime. Up in Concord, New Hampshire, in the farmhouse in which she finally settled in 1892, she had a relatively calm life compared with the Boston years. Here she took the steps that led to establishing her church on a basis that would allow it to encompass the world. She began to think about better ways to reach the world beyond Boston and even beyond the United States. In the last decade of her life she found the movement getting well established in England and starting in Germany and France. Finally, besides the religious publications she started, she had her directors in Boston begin the publication in 1908 of the *Christian Science Monitor* as a daily, nonsectarian, general interest newspaper with news about the entire world.

One may look at the last twenty years of Mrs. Eddy's life as a period in which she completed the organizational work that marks her as the founder of her movement as well as its discoverer. One may also look at the entire forty-four years that elapsed from 1866 to her passing in 1910 as the outward expansion of the thought of the first Christian Scientist. They compose one of the most remarkable stories of any human being. It is ironic that in America, where the feminist movement has been so vocal, the interests of feminists have on the whole been so juridical in orientation that they have so far bypassed the greatness of this woman. Quite apart from the ultimate judgment on her interpretation of Christianity (while recognizing it as a serious and internally consistent system), her tenacity, conviction, courage—and success—would long ago have made her a cult hero of the feminists. It is perhaps fortunate for the cause of Christian Science itself that she has been denied this kind of passing fame.

✳ ✳ ✳

Up to this point we have seen that surveys of contemporary American views on religion validate William James's contention that the physical sciences cannot replace the important role that religion plays in life. We have seen that there remains an important attachment to

Christianity, even though few people seem to have a deep concept of the lessons of the Bible. At the same time, developments in the sciences have made us aware that reality can be described in more than one way—and depending on how we describe it, or see it, we may open up new experiences (as with the world of electrons). The survey of the early Church, though not meant to be a history of theology, indicated that unanimity did not exist at the start as to what was at the heart of the Christian message, and that the development of the Church itself somewhat changed the emphasis of that message over the years. The chapter on discovery showed how new models, or paradigms, are occasionally called for to fit the facts that are being observed. It is the thesis of this book that Christian Science is the called-for paradigm of Christianity today. And now that we have seen in this chapter how some of the thought trends of the nineteenth century and specific events of Mrs. Eddy's own life acted to make her the discoverer of this paradigm, we have the necessary context for looking at Christian Science. It is now time to consider the articulation Mrs. Eddy gave to her discovery of, as she called it, a new-old Christianity.

Chapter 7

THE METAPHYSICS
OF CHRISTIAN SCIENCE

GOD

The metaphysical system of Christian Science begins with God. Everything that Mrs. Eddy had to say in the development of her theology stemmed from her definition of God. The definition itself is simple enough—largely a group of synonyms modified by a few descriptive adjectives. Before discussing these synonyms, however, one must caution that words alone are obviously not enough. Words— especially simple ones like "love"—mean different things to different people. Words not translatable into actions are not alive enough to argue over anyhow. In James's lectures at Edinburgh, he spoke very highly of transcendent Christian *experiences*, but had few good things to say about metaphysical statements that did not seem to him to connect with discernible cause and effect in human experience. Mrs. Eddy would have agreed, had she been aware of what the intellectual connoisseurs of the religious experience were saying. Instead, she was "in the trenches" herself for nearly half a century, working out the means by which others could learn the road to spirituality.

As a matter of fact, her writing about Christian Science came only after she had discovered and demonstrated its effectiveness in healing others. Her earliest students commented that her teaching was imbued with a spirit that was far ahead of what she was able, at least at first, to express in her writings on the subject. She had no intellectual or even theological interest in constructing a system of metaphysics per se. She had discovered the way to demonstrate God's presence here, to have some sense that the kingdom of heaven means a perfect spiritual order already in existence, an order that, when understood, overrides and overrules anything in human experience that would deny it. This discovery included within it her ability to articulate it in language that would be understandable to succeeding generations.

Many people know that Christian Scientists, as a matter of normal practice, spend considerable amounts of time reading the Bible and their textbook, as well as the periodical literature published by the Christian Science Publishing Society. Therefore they may have the false impression that Christian Science is primarily introspective or meditative, and not given to action. To be practiced consistently and with some degree of success, it is correct that the metaphysics of Christian Science does need to be accurately stated. But its basic statement is a simple one. Any difficulty an average person in today's world has in working in Christian Science would probably stem less from a misunderstanding of its theology than from an attempt to accommodate it to the widespread beliefs in human thought that it contradicts. The natural tendency of the human mind, until it has become accustomed to thinking in spiritual terms of reference, is to make some accommodation for the old beliefs of materiality along with the light that is coming in from a new source. It would be akin to using some of the laws of Newton in the same problem one was trying to work out with quantum mechanics. The metaphysics must be practiced with singleness of thought. To refer to the concept of different paradigms, we can work with only one paradigm or model at a time.

It is always the application of what one thinks he or she knows of the theology of Christian Science that is important, not self-centered study alone. "The song of Christian Science," Mrs. Eddy wrote to her church members in 1900, "is 'Work—work—work—watch and pray.' The close observer reports three types of human nature—the right thinker and worker, the idler, and the intermediate."[1] Given her own earnestness and diligence, she had no more patience with the "intermediate" than with the "idler." The practice of Christian Science requires both study and prayer, but the aim of both is some evidence of change in human thought and experience. Meditation is no end in itself.

Yet the words that describe God have a meaning that expands throughout the lifetime of one using them. Mrs. Eddy ascribed seven major descriptive synonyms to God, six of which are found in abundance in the Bible: Life, Truth, Love, Spirit, Soul, and Mind. A seventh, Principle, is implied in the Bible in the sense that God is often spoken of as the ultimate lawgiver and as unchanging. (Whenever these words are used in their deific meaning, they are capitalized.) She also speaks of God as All. His allness is not synonymous with the philosopher's pantheism, however, since pantheism finds God present in physical nature. The universe Mrs. Eddy was trying to describe in normal language is one of Spirit. God as Spirit could not be conceived of as being in the natural world; neither, for that matter, is he in his spiritual creation, although the creation can be conceived of as being inseparable from its Creator.

Her definition of God in the glossary of *Science and Health* says in its entirety: "the great I AM; the all-knowing, all-seeing, all-acting, all-wise, all-loving, and eternal; Principle; Mind; Soul; Spirit; Life; Truth; Love; all substance; intelligence."[2]

The particular synonyms that Mrs. Eddy used for God are inclusive terms. God is not in seven parts (any more than he is in three). The Mind that is God is also infinite Love, for instance. To think about God in terms of these biblical synonyms, to apply the qualities of one to the other, is to begin to enlarge one's human sense of what the Bible means when it says, "the Lord he is God in heaven above, and upon the earth beneath: there is none else."[3] One can use the synonyms, such as in contemplating the qualities attributable to each one and what their presence means in his or her experience, in almost endless ways. Again, the words themselves are not the be-all and end-all. They are the starting point, from which the reality of God appears to human consciousness in a way that makes it act differently. The definition of God can only tell us *about* God; the Christian's goal is to have some direct experience of God's presence.

Mind as one synonym for God is a starting point for many Christian Scientists in any discussion of God. It is one way of establishing in thought the fact that if God is Mind, or infinite intelligence, his universe is a creation of ideas, not of material objects. Mind as used in Christian Science is also one of the words most misunderstood by those who have only a peripheral acquaintance with the terminology of Christian Science. When I hear someone say he has always believed in the power of mind over matter, I cringe a bit. It is the human mind, which is alleged to have this power to control matter, that Mrs. Eddy identified as the very antithesis of God. It was the operation of the human mind in terms of mesmerism and suggestion, which she had experienced with Phineas Quimby, that had shown her the vast separation between this limited human mentality and the divine intelligence. That the human mind does exert considerable influence over the body is more generally accepted today, and this will be discussed more in the next chapter on the practice of Christian Science. But Mrs. Eddy fully accepted Paul's statement that "the carnal mind is enmity against God."[4] Her Mind is a divine Mind, an infinite intelligence that is the cause of every manifestation of true intelligence in the universe.

The activity of this divine Mind is synonymous with Life. God is not a static being. He is the fountain of all life. The Gospel of John starts with: "In the beginning was the Word, and the Word was with God, and the Word was God. The same was in the beginning with God. . . . In him was life; and the life was the light of men."

What is God's relationship to what he has created? Love alone can express this aspect of the nature of God. It is a love that includes the highest human sense of compassion, although divine Love, God, can perhaps be best glimpsed from our human standpoint as the wholeness, completeness, perfection, and oneness or unity of all that God beholds—and he sees all that he has made. All is held and maintained under the loving control of the eternal Father-Mother. Mrs. Eddy consistently referred to God as both Father and Mother, using the compound word "Father-Mother." This inclusive parental term emphasizes that man has one complete spiritual parent, which certainly includes the nurturing qualities of motherly love. It includes the Lawgiver of the Old Testament, but also the compassion that Jesus exemplified and the exalted sense of God that is described in 1 John.

Spirit suggests the omnipresence of God. The psalmist had written more than two thousand years ago, "Whither shall I flee from thy presence?"[5] Returning to the other synonyms, if God, Spirit, is everpresent, then Love is everywhere, the expression of intelligence is everywhere, and so on. So are all the attributes that one can apply to these single-word definitions of God. Moreover, if Spirit is everywhere, the substance of everything that exists must be spiritual.

The Bible uses the word *soul* in two different senses. It more frequently refers to soul as the struggling conscience within man, trying to escape from sin but at the same time also the essential core of man's being. Mrs. Eddy saw God as the source and center of the individual's being, and found in some Bible passages the identification of soul with God. Hence, as a synonym for God, Soul suggests the inseparable relationship the individual has with God, a relationship that is the basis of man's individual identity. Since Soul, or God, is individually expressed, all the colorful variations of individuality are found in Soul.

That leaves Principle and Truth, two words that have some degree of coincidence even with each other. Truth may bring to mind the Bible verse, "A God of truth . . ."[6] or Pilate's question to Jesus, "What is truth?"[7] One line of thought that suggests itself is that a God who is Truth and is omnipotent can neither make error nor be aware of error *nor allow its existence*, and we shall discuss this further along in more detail.

Principle certainly brings to mind the unchanging nature of God, as well as his function as the ultimate lawgiver. When we think of the "will" of God, for instance, this is not will in the same sense as human will might be considered. God's will is *law*.

Is God really a he? Of course not. But is God a she? In one of the early editions of the Christian Science textbook, Mrs. Eddy experimented with the pronoun, calling God "she." But she quickly reverted to the more conventional "he." Mrs. Eddy does frequently refer to God as Father-Mother, however, indicating by this that God's qualities include all those associated with motherhood as well as fatherhood.

One might more properly ask, Is God a person at all? Mrs. Eddy dealt with this question in various ways, but what means most is not the linguistics involved but the attempt to express in human language, with the only terms available, the nature of the infinite power that none of us as individual human beings can expect to totally comprehend.

In a small booklet published in the late 1880s, called *No and Yes*, Mrs. Eddy responded to many of the questions that were then being asked about Christian Science. One of them was: "Is there a personal deity?" She answered, in part: "God is Love; and Love is Principle, not person. What the person of the infinite is, we know not; but we are gratefully and lovingly conscious of the fatherliness of this Supreme Being. God is individual, and man is His individualized idea."[8] Later in the same answer she stated: "Person is formed after the manner of mortal man, so far as he can conceive of personality. Limitless personality is inconceivable. . . . Error would fashion Deity in a manlike mould, while Truth is moulding a Godlike man."[9]

This would seem to indicate that it is not helpful to think of God as a person, at least not in the same way that we think of each other. Yet neither does the description of him in cold, monosyllabic terms begin to catch the grandeur and majesty of the eternal, unchanging, and benign power that Mrs. Eddy saw holding the universe in its grasp. It is interesting that in her letters and informal remarks she continued to speak of God as talking to her, just as he is supposed to have talked to his prophets in the Bible.

The kind of God Mrs. Eddy found in Christian Science cannot be described in language only. However, by using the terminology she evolved over some period of time in her statement of Christian Science, Christian Scientists find that they have a fuller sense of God. Mrs. Eddy, as an adolescent, had rejected the Calvinist concept of a God who chose some to be saved and condemned others to eternal hellfire. Her mother's sense of God had included the comfort of a loving parent. Mrs. Eddy herself most often combined the two synonyms Love and Principle, perhaps indicating the degree to which the sense of God as Love must permeate any approach to deity. The two words also combine most clearly what human experience would call the feminine and the masculine elements of God—the compassionate tenderness of the mother and the law-giving, law-enforcing role of the father. On the other hand, she never departed from the awesome sense of deity, that "blazing sun of glory," that Calvinism had presented to her in her Congregational church upbringing.

Again, she made the best possible use she could of the human terms available to her. However, talking about God in terms of a group of simple synonyms should not be construed as a tight bundle of nouns that tell us all about God. Consistency in living with the thought that God is All and that such words as Life, Truth, and Love express his nature takes time to cultivate. It is this process of learning to live closer to God, to have an abiding sense of his presence, that makes the practical difference. "God, good," she wrote, "is self-existent and self-expressed, though indefinable as a whole."[10]

Some current theology approaches God in terms of his being a verb in addition to his being a noun. The Canadian scholar Northrop Frye says in his book *The Great Code:*

> In Exodus 3:14, though God also gives himself a name, he defines himself . . . as "I am that I am," which scholars say is more accurately rendered "I will be what I will be." That is, we might come closer to what is meant in the Bible by the word "God" if we understood it as a verb, and not a verb of simple asserted existence but a verb implying a process accomplishing itself.[11]

This position is not inconsistent with Mrs. Eddy's definition, since a natural follow-through for the person working with the synonyms for God is to ask of himself or herself, "All right, if God is Principle or God is Mind, what is Principle or Mind *doing?* What is the activity of God I need to identify as present right here?"

MAN

The only reality, then, that Christian Science recognizes is an all-encompassing deity, embracing and including man and the universe as its reflection or expression. Since God is divine Mind, one way Mrs. Eddy used to describe man was as idea. Words, again, but words that could be used to make the relationship of man to God more real, more usable. They suggest that man is formed wholly by God and included in the divine Mind as an inseparable idea. Since God includes all, man by reflection expresses the qualities and attributes of God. Each of the synonyms, and the qualities that characterize them, can be developed to see the fullness of man. But this man is the ideal man, the man who already exists but that human beings must grow into. Her terminology was more precise than that of Paul, but the thought was the same as Paul expressed it in writing to the Ephesians: "Till we all come in the unity of the faith, and of the knowledge of the Son of God, unto a perfect man, unto the measure of the stature of the fulness of Christ."[12]

The realization of what constitutes man is plainly work that suggests the possibility of infinite progression. It involves overcoming, growing out of, error—which has not yet been discussed here. The purpose of the metaphysics of Christian Science is to give to human thought the systematic aid it requires to grasp the truth of being and, by degrees, to demonstrate the presence of the kingdom of God in everyday experience. The task, as well as the promise, before the human being is summed up thusly by Mrs. Eddy:

> Mortals have a very imperfect sense of the spiritual man and of the infinite range of his thought. To him belongs eternal Life. Never born and never dying, it were impossible for man, under the government of God in eternal Science, to fall from his high estate.[13]

or:

> Mortals are not like immortals, created in God's own image; but infinite Spirit being all, mortal consciousness will at last yield to the scientific fact and disappear, and the real sense of being, perfect and forever intact, will appear.[14]

MATTER AND EVIL; THE TWO GENESIS STORIES OF CREATION

It was from Mrs. Eddy's sense of God's allness that the positions of Christian Science regarding the nothingness of matter and error stem. Stated in all their nakedness, they are an affront to the everyday experience of the physical senses on which we rely, as well as to human history, which is one massive record of good and evil in combination.

Mrs. Eddy did not begin, however, with the nothingness of matter and evil. She began with God. And if God really is all, she reasoned, then there is no place in a spiritual universe for the limitations of matter. And if God, Truth, is really in control, evil does not have any realm of its own in which to operate. Having gone this far, how did she explain the seeming existence of matter and evil?

She followed a logic unique to her. They could not exist, she maintained, except in an incorrect, inaccurate concept of existence, which she denominated mortal mind. (She sometimes refers to this inaccurate statement of existence as a dream state.) This passage from *Science and Health* sums it up well: If we give power to matter, she argued, we were "disown[ing] the Almighty."

> To seize the first horn of this dilemma and consider matter as a power in and of itself, is to leave the creator out of His own universe; while to grasp the other horn of the dilemma and regard God as the creator of matter, is not only to make Him responsible for all disasters, physical and moral, but to announce Him as their source, thereby making Him guilty of maintaining perpetual misrule in the form and under the name of natural law.[15]

Parts of this position were not unique to her, but the totality *and the implications she drew therefrom* certainly were. Some Roman Catholic theologians during the Middle Ages had dealt with evil, or error, as the absence of good, having no entity of its own. Augustine, for example, argued in the fourth century against the Manichean heresy, which maintained the existence of both a kingdom of light and a kingdom of darkness. However, it was one thing to deal with evil as nothing philosophically and another to see how to demonstrate this in individual experience. Mrs. Eddy's discovery put the latter within the realm of possibility for ordinary people.

As for matter, even in the early days of the Church, its theologians had been aware of the Greek position regarding matter. Plato had taught that the material universe coexisted with the spiritual force, or intelligence, which gave it form and meaning. (He did not actually call this spiritual force God, however.) One of the earliest theologians to deal with the problem of matter in Western philosophy, Clement of Alexandria, realized the contradiction implied in a God who coexisted with preexistent matter.

> Apologists like Clement, Theophilus, and Tertullian recognized that the coeternity of God and matter was inconsistent with the sovereignty and freedom of God. In spite of the difficulties raised by the doctrine of creation ex nihilo for any attempt to cope with the problem of evil, the alternative to this doctrine appeared to be a pantheism which taught that "God and matter are the same, two names for one thing" or a dualism that could be resolved, if at all, by denying that God the Creator "made all things freely."[16]

Mrs. Eddy was aware of the distinction between the two creation stories in Genesis. She saw the story as told in the first chapter of Genesis as the true story; for her it was the story of the unfoldment of an entirely spiritual universe. Each of the elements of creation are seen in Christian Science as ideas of God, with the highest element, man, appearing at the apex of creation. This man is wholly spiritual. Having been created in a state of perfection by a God who controls all, it would be impossible for this man to fall from his perfect being.

It is in the second chapter of Genesis, when the mists of error rise up, that a false sense, a material sense, of creation, arises. But in the theology of Christian Science this is not creation; it is not, within the metaphysical framework or paradigm of Christian Science, even real. But it does need to be challenged and disproved in human experience. It is a mirage that progressively loses its power to deceive us as we dwell in thought on the real man, who can also be called the individual representation of Christ. It was such a moment of spiritual vision, centered around her recollection of a healing of Jesus, that healed Mrs. Eddy of injuries from her serious fall in 1866.

This sounds reminiscent of some of the earlier discussion (including but not limited to the gnostics) about the nature of the creation during the first two centuries of Christianity. Many of the early Christians worked within a mind-set that was heavily influenced by Greek philosophical concepts. Plato had described a kind of demiurge that was responsible for the creation of the material universe. The early Church theologians rejected this concept, for it made two eternal powers necessary—God and the demiurge. If matter was eternal, then an all-powerful God was not the only power in the universe. So they settled on the second option: God had created matter out of nothing. This left God in control but did not solve the next problem: how to explain the deficiencies of matter, its changeability, the mortality of material life, and so on.

Mrs. Eddy realized the dilemma. In her chapter in *Science and Health* called "Science of Being," she threw down the gauntlet:

> The theories I combat are these: (1) that all is matter; (2) that matter originates in Mind, and is as real as Mind, possessing intelligence and life. The first theory, that matter is everything, is quite as reasonable as the second, that Mind and matter coexist and cooperate. One only of the following statements is true: (1) that everything is matter; (2) that everything is Mind. Which one is it?[17]

The twentieth century may seem to have resolved that question in favor of matter, even though what seemed to be matter one hundred years ago has undergone one subdivision after another by theoretical physicists, until matter is now defined as units of energy. However, the processes of scientific research have tended to enthrone the material senses and their extensions—the mathematical constructs of the human mind. As noted in chapter 3, the position of the physical sciences has left less space—certainly not within their own framework, or paradigm—for any transcendent view of existence. At the same time, and more hopefully, the growing concept or recognition that there can be more than one way to view reality at least opens up to human thought the possibility of a discussion of spiritual laws and a single spiritual source of those laws.

Now, it may seem entirely illogical to say that everything is Mind, or God and his manifestation, as Christian Science teaches. And it *is* illogical to the mortal existence that is itself part of the mind-matter continuum that Christian Science calls unreal. Mrs. Eddy was aware of this, and did not waste many words in philosophizing about the supposed contradiction of the material senses. Demonstration in some degree of the truth of her revelation was the only practical answer to those who challenged her sense of God's allness.

Even the separation of a discussion of the theology of Christian Science from its practice, as in this chapter and the following one, is somewhat artificial. It is the practice, the individual's seeing his own evidence of the usefulness of the theology, that confirms it in individual thought as being a correct statement of the science of being. Mrs. Eddy herself had little patience for or interest in the letter without its demonstration. In answer to a rather convoluted question relating to this, she had a terse reply (not all of it quoted here):

> Is not the basis of Mind-healing a destruction of the evidence of the material senses, and restoration of the true evidence of spiritual sense?
>
> It is, so far as you perceive and understand this predicate and postulate of Mind-healing; but the Science of Mind-healing is best understood in practical demonstration. The proof of what you apprehend, in the simplest definite and absolute form of healing, can alone answer this question of how much you understand of Christian Science Mind-healing.[18]

Christian Science often uses the words *matter* and *evil* together; they were also often linked in the writings of the early church fathers. They are not, however, synonymous. Any sense of separation from God is evil, and the cause of that separation must be overcome for the evil to cease. Evil, in turn, arises from mankind's *belief* in the reality of matter. It is not that matter itself is evil. But acceptance of its reality in human thought results in the sense of separation from God, good, as well as in the belief in separate, limited mentalities. It results in the belief in limited good, since matter in any of its manifestations is limited. And belief in material life includes the belief in death—again, an evidence of matter's inherent limits.

Some of the gnostic and other early Christian writers looked on the material universe as evil. The position that Christian Science takes, that the material universe is a mistaken view of reality, has an entirely different result in terms of the human activity that follows. If one looks on matter as evil, one outcome of this can be the life that turns away from anything to do with the existential world about us. An extreme asceticism, which even has no use for procreation, is one such result, and there were such sects among some of the early Christians. Yet we have seen that the questions the gnostics raised about the position of matter also had some biblical roots. Paul's statement that "we know that if our earthly house of this tabernacle were dissolved, we have a building of God, an house not made with hands, eternal in the heavens"[19] can be taken as a statement of Christian orthodoxy, as proof that gnosticism itself was present and accepted as part of the Christian gospel, or as a statement of Christian Science. The most interesting interpretation is that all three possibilities are simultaneously true!

Mrs. Eddy did not see the material universe as evil as much as reflecting the present state of thought of those looking at it. "The physical universe reflects the conscious and unconscious thoughts of mortals."[20] It is ultimately unreal, but it is, in terms of the human perception of it, also plastic—it is molded according to the thinking brought to bear on it by each individual. Thus a Christian Scientist does not turn away from it, but he sees how much his own adoption of the model of creation outlined in the first chapter of Genesis can do to bring his present sense of existence, which inevitably includes the consciousness of a material world, more in line with what he accepts into his own consciousness of spiritual reality.

CHRIST JESUS

Having defined man as the perfect reflection, or child, of God, what is the place of Christ Jesus in Christian Science? Is there a need for a savior, for a mediator (as Paul calls him) between man and his Maker? From the first of her jottings that occurred after her conversations with Quimby, Mrs. Eddy seems to have had a clear understanding of the distinction between the human Jesus and the eternal Christ that he represented. It was a distinction joined by an inseparable relationship! She wrote, for example: "The invisible Christ was imperceptible to the so-called personal senses, whereas Jesus appeared as a bodily existence."[21] Not a student of ancient Bible history or the history of the early Church (although she had undoubtedly read books about the early centuries), her language pierced the layers of scholastic theology that had clung to the person of Christ Jesus.

A child of the Bible, she fully accepted the Bible story of his life as literally true. He was born of a virgin. He performed "miracles" as a matter of everyday living. He was crucified; yet he rose from the grave. After being physically seen by his disciples for a few weeks, he rose out of their "physical apprehension," as she phrases it. At this point she departs from orthodox theology, both Roman Catholic and most Protestant, to say that his life was an example for us. His life was more than *an* example, however, and herein lies the difference between Christian Science and some forms of liberal Protestantism. His life was the consummate example, and there will never be another entirely like it, she maintained. The crucifixion and resurrection experience, while not an expiation for the sins of mankind, were nevertheless a vital part and the climax of his mission. They "served to uplift faith to understand eternal Life, even the allness of Soul, Spirit, and the nothingness of matter," she wrote.[22]

Viewing creation as wholly spiritual, Mrs. Eddy took a different view of sin than did orthodox theologians. She wrote once that people took either too big or too little a view of sin. Never condoning the perpetuation of any personal error in a human being's life, she nevertheless saw sin in its big sense. Sin was a mortal belief in separation from God, from infinite good. Believing the first chapter of Genesis to be the correct account of creation, if taken in the sense of a universe of spiritual unfoldment, she saw in the older folk myth of the second and third chapters something quite different from Augustine's version of original sin descending from Adam's transgression. She saw belief stemming from the tree of knowledge as being hopelessly flawed, since its core combined a knowledge of good and evil, of a creation in other words in which it was possible for man to be separated from God. "The first impression material man had of himself was one of nakedness and shame. Had he lost man's rich inheritance and God's behest, dominion over all the earth? No! This had never been bestowed on Adam."[23]

Man's salvation lay in finding his relation to God and living it. This was what Jesus had done. Because of the manner of his birth, however, he had been freer to claim and experience what it meant to be the son of God, even though he also experienced every manner of temptation. He thus could make a full demonstration of his manhood as the perfect child of God, the Christ, during the brief years of his ministry.

There was no problem for Mrs. Eddy in comparing the synoptic Gospels with the Gospel of John. She did not have the academic training to let her worry about whether the Word in John was John's accommodation to the Greeks' sense of the Logos as creator. The Gospels were *all* necessary to tell the story. That John set forth the role of Jesus as the Christ is not even specially mentioned by her. And for Christian Scientists studying her writings in conjunction with the Bible, but particularly the New Testament, there appear numerous enough references in the letters of Paul to indicate that he also (at least part of the time, and maybe depending on whom he was writing) saw the Christ as distinct from the earthly life of Jesus. There are also some current scholars who do not think that John's use of the Logos was in deference to Greek thought at all.

At the same time, Mrs. Eddy did not take the vague position of the gnostics regarding the man Jesus. Jesus was a specific human being who stood at a certain point in history and performed concrete acts. Others would in increasing measure demonstrate the Christ, the real man, as their selfhood too, but no one on the time line of history could or would ever stand in the role of Christ Jesus. Even though the freer intellectual world of New England Unitarianism, and of Emerson and the transcendentalists, had prepared the way for a more open examination of religion, Mrs. Eddy was much closer to orthodox Christianity on this score than she was to the looser interpretations of Jesus' life among the Unitarians and transcendentalists.

One can also understand, having the concept of God that Mrs. Eddy entertained, how she could not bring the orthodox concept of the Christian Trinity into Christian Science. The uniqueness of Jesus, yes, and the holy nature of that process by which the knowledge of God and his Christ comes to the individual, which the churches have traditionally called the Holy Spirit or Holy Ghost—these she appreciated with all the devotion of an orthodox, evangelical Christian. But she could have these without invading the concept of an all-powerful, "jealous" God who had first revealed his nature to the Jewish patriarchs. One could have the same reverence toward Jesus as a unique character in history and feel for the suffering he endured on the cross, but still look upon him as a human being. In fact, perceiving him as another human being placed a heavier burden, and greater individual responsibility, on his followers—us—to live with some measure of the dominion he showed through his own life.

If it were not for differences in words caused in large part by the different cosmology held by the early Christians, the position of Christian Science regarding Jesus would seem closer to orthodoxy than it does. The entire discussion about the Godhead, with Jesus as part of a triune God, took place close to two millennia ago. It was all too easy at that time to formulate theories that seemed to imply a God made in the image of mortal man.

On the other hand, Christian Science burst upon the world at an opportune moment. Not only were political and social conditions in the United States conducive to at least allowing a religious experiment that included physical healing as part of its practice. The mental climate also saw all phenomena increasingly in terms of cause and effect, or chains of activity that could be explained and repeated. The average person was approaching in his own mode of thinking the orderly thought processes of the sciences. Thus, anyone having the concept Mrs. Eddy had of an omnipotent God, including his benevolence toward his creation and his everpresence, would have had a harder time thinking of a triune God in any but a poetic sense.

Perhaps the closest analogy to the Christian Science position on Jesus that has come to my attention is in a conversation a Rutgers philosophy professor, Renee Weber, had with a converted Roman Catholic priest, English by origin, living in an ashram in India. Weber raised the question somewhat irreverently, "Was Jesus a man or a fish? If it's a fish, it's another order of species, and there is little hope for us. If it was a man, then potentially it can be learned by anyone."

To this somewhat bizarre manner of posing the question, Father Griffiths responded that Jesus must be seen as a man.

> To me one of the great weaknesses in modern Christianity is that really almost from the time of the Council of Nicea in the fourth century, Jesus has moved over from the human to the divine. He belonged to this humanity, and he had the body of a Jew and the psyche of a Jew, and he belonged to his time. In that sense he was totally human and he shares the whole human reality, including suffering and death. In him as in all, there is the capacity for self-transcendence. But in him, as I understand it, that capacity was unlimited.[24]

Christian Science expresses it similarly, and has been doing so for over one hundred years. Jesus fully demonstrated the Christ, his spiritual selfhood. This Christ was the selfhood Jesus identified with when he said, "Before Abraham was, I am."[25] His consciousness of being the Christ, or expressing Christ, was the spiritual connection with the divine presence, or his Father, which explained his healing works, including his own resurrection and ascension.

This is far more than a dry academic distinction. If Jesus is seen and understood as the supreme example in human history, his life can give to every one of his followers the motivation to learn what it was that Jesus knew and to follow him in a practical way—a way that in Christian Science is frequently talked about as "demonstration."

Living in India for half a lifetime, Father Griffiths has also had to deal with the dilemma Christians face of having their religion regarded as Western. Although the Bible lands were on the western edge of Asia, the spread of Christianity took place largely in the West, and Western civilization is very largely the combined development of Greek thought, Roman law, and Judeo-Christian ideals in history. Given the near destruction of that civilization in the brutal wars of the first half of the twentieth century, this may seem at best a dubious commendation for Christianity. There is, nevertheless, an identification between those peoples who *said* they practiced Christianity and Western civilization that cannot be avoided. In any case, Christianity has had trouble getting even a hearing in some other cultures, both because of the confusing doctrine of the Trinity, with its emphasis on the divinity of Christ Jesus, and because of its identification with the West.

Could there be another individual like Jesus? Weber asked Father Griffiths. His reply:

> In the Christian understanding we would say, no. It was a particular historic revelation, it came to a definite historic end and finality in Jesus, and the total reality is realized there; but that is not denying that the divine mystery is revealing itself in all different religions, in all different human experiences. But they are all related to this final eschatological event.[26]

This is the same answer Christian Science gives to that question. And, it would say, Jesus and Christianity are certainly not events that belong to the West. His life and its meaning for mankind is universal. Yet it was necessary for its particularity to be demonstrated by one man—Christ Jesus.

SALVATION

One final element in the metaphysical system of Christian Science remains to be discussed. And it leads into the next chapter on the practice of Christian Science. Metaphysics deals with the nature of reality, and we have seen that in the metaphysical system of Christian Science, reality is wholly spiritual. Mrs. Eddy found a complete description of God and his universe in the first chapter of Genesis, as she understood it.

There remains that second chapter of Genesis, however, the false concept of reality, the mirage, the illusion of man as a creator or cocreator with God of a material universe, and the fall of man into sin. Although Christian Science does not accept any part of this allegory about man as being true in an absolute spiritual sense, this and the succeeding chapters of Genesis present the phenomenal world, the mixture of good and evil, that we human beings have to deal with. And Mrs. Eddy knew that too. The difference between her approach and that of orthodox Christian theology, or for that matter all the philosophies of the ages, was to show by demonstration that this false sense of creation really is false. She saw the role of Christ Jesus as one of showing by example how to restore the real man and the real universe.

Now, if one is false and the other is true, what is the connection? There can be no connection in the realm of Spirit, of God, as God is ignorant of that which does not have actual existence. The connection is in the human consciousness that is a mixture of the false claims of mortal mind and some awareness of the Christ, or real man, that belongs to everyone as his or her spiritual identity. Salvation, then, consists in putting off the old man, to use Paul's phrase, and putting on the new man. One is not battling against a material universe or a material man; he or she is simply exchanging the false belief in such a universe or such a man for what is spiritually true about man right now. One of the ways in which Mrs. Eddy describes this process in *Science and Health* reads:

> The manifestation of God through mortals is as light passing through the window-pane. The light and the glass never mingle, but as matter the glass is less opaque than the walls. The mortal mind through which Truth appears most vividly is that one which has lost much materiality—much error—in order to become a better transparency for Truth. Then, like a cloud melting into thin vapor, it no longer hides the sun.[27]

Man's salvation lies in knowing and demonstrating Truth. This happens in the realm of consciousness and in the world of action. Having got this far, it should now be clear that salvation in Christian Science is much closer to the gnostic position of knowledge (but not secret knowledge!) than to the set of passive doctrinal beliefs that came to identify one as a Christian. Jesus' role is then illumined as that of exemplar and way-shower, but not that of a personal savior. It would be impossible for someone else to do our work for us. If one is suffering from a wrong concept of reality, the only way to remove that suffering and its effects is to replace the wrong concept with the right one. Among the many meanings that Christians have given to the term *grace*, one of them is the acceptance of God's love for man. That is ultimately what is involved in salvation—simply being willing to learn and to accept, without any mental reservation, what is already true of our real identity.

In discussing what the early Church had meant by the term *salvation*, Pelikan raises but does not answer a point that is essential in understanding the message of Christian Science. He says:

> There is, in fact, an even deeper, though largely unexamined, ambiguity in the doctrine of salvation through Christ. . . . Was the work of Christ to be thought of as having accomplished the reconciliation between God and the world *or as having disclosed a reconciliation that had actually been there all along?* That ambiguity was especially palpable when the work of Christ was represented as that of the exemplar and teacher who brought the true revelation of God's will to man.[28]

To comment on that with the broadest brush strokes, which are bound not to cover every theological wrinkle in the two-thousand-year history of Christian theology, the Catholic church as well as the Protestant Reformation saw the work of Christ Jesus as accomplishing the reconciliation of man with God. Mrs. Eddy saw it as the latter—the reconciliation has existed since the creation of man, but the life and works of Christ Jesus were the first as well as final example to the rest of mankind of the fact of reconciliation.

This reconciliation, or each person's own demonstration of man's at-one-ment with God, takes place in consciousness. In studying the textbook, one finds that Mrs. Eddy generally employs the term *mortal mind* to stand for the generalized belief in life and intelligence in matter. She does, however, also talk about mortal mind in the sense of the individual's own thought—usually an unenlightened thought. Human consciousness is a step higher. It includes some of the beliefs of mortal mind, but it is also aware of the Christ, Truth, to some extent. A purely spiritual consciousness, on the other hand, would be the demonstration of absolute reality, in which man is conscious of nothing but God's thoughts flowing through him, as it were.

Science and Health contains one explicit outline of this step-by-step process of salvation, but it lies implicit in the words of almost every page of the book. Explicitly stated, it reads:

Scientific Translation of Mortal Mind

FIRST DEGREE: DEPRAVITY.

Physical. Evil beliefs, passions and appetites, fear, depraved will, self-justification, pride, envy, deceit, hatred, revenge, sin, sickness, disease, death.

SECOND DEGREE: EVIL BELIEFS DISAPPEARING.

Moral. Humanity, honesty, affection, compassion, hope, faith, meekness, temperance.

THIRD DEGREE: UNDERSTANDING.

Spiritual. Wisdom, purity, spiritual understanding, spiritual power, love, health, holiness.[29]

Mrs. Eddy did not present Christian Science as just another religious denomination with a series of doctrinal beliefs. She developed the metaphysical statement as an aid to spiritual understanding, to give her students an opportunity to practice Christianity as it had been practiced by Christ Jesus. Her religion was not only a returning home to the new birth Christianity provides in the sense of restoring physical healing as an integral element of salvation. It was, even more, to restore Christianity to all Christians as a practice, a way of living, and to remove it from the realm of theory and Sunday sermons that it was for many people in her day. So it is now time to consider what Christian Scientists mean by that word "practice."

Chapter 8

THE PRACTICE
OF CHRISTIAN SCIENCE

The first chapter of this book suggested that one could not really understand the concept of practice in Christian Science without some effort at *doing* it—that is, practicing it for oneself. It is analogous, I said, to reading a book about how to swim but not actually getting in the water to try it. But here we are, at the water's edge; shall we at least look at it together?

The preceding chapter discussed some of the basic concepts common to all monotheistic religions, but most particularly to Christianity: the nature of God, the nature of man, the problem of evil and the nature of matter, man's seeming alienation from the kingdom of heaven, and the role of Christ Jesus in showing him the way back to it. Yet none of these concepts, merely expressed intellectually, gets us back to heaven or finds us in it, unless our own consciousness reacts to religious truth and is somehow and in some measure changed by it.

The only way one really learns about the practice of Christian Science is to do it—that is, to practice. As theory, Christian Science has a consistent internal logic. But that is still only theory. The practice of Christian Science in individual experience is the ultimate test of its truth—and utility—as religion. Does it meet those tests we talked about earlier that make it the core of one's everyday experience?

If reading about practice alone will not do it, there is still a major reason to write about it here. It is to clarify mistaken concepts of what the practice is, and to show that Mrs. Eddy's development of the method of practice in Christian Science was closely linked to the healing practice of Jesus.

I had an uncle who was a kind of nonpracticing Christian Scientist. A second-generation German-American, he enlisted in the U.S. Navy in the First World War to demonstrate his unconditional loyalty to America. Assigned to a troop ship, he made several crossings of the Atlantic during the course of America's participation in that war. He had been raised in the Missouri Synod of the Lutheran church, and my grandmother's letters tried to give him spiritual comfort while he was crisscrossing the Atlantic Ocean. She wrote to him in April 1918, "I was very happy to read you took holy communion on ship, because you know without writing you this, that if we do right as far as we know in this world, we have nothing to fear for the other."

What gave him the most comfort, however, was getting to know another sailor who worked in the boiler room of the ship. This man, a Christian Scientist, was the most fearless person my uncle met on board ship, and he would often find him sitting reading a copy of *Science and Health*, even in the boiler room. After the war was over, my uncle began to study Christian Science and go to church services in Chicago. He had many healings in Christian Science throughout a very long life and only used the services of a doctor once, when, in his eighties, he had a cataract removed. Yet, I would say that he never really learned to practice Christian Science. (And, while I found him one of my most interesting relatives, it was not his example that roused my own interest in Christian Science.) He used the services of a Christian Science practitioner often, but he complained to me after I had become interested in Science as a young college student, "You know, the trouble with *Science and Health* is that Mrs. Eddy never told us how to give a treatment."

Of course Mrs. Eddy instructed her students how to give a treatment, just as she told them a lot about God. But just as there is no simple definition of God, which alone brings an individual to experiencing God's presence, likewise there is no formula for a treatment, or prayer. We find ourselves back at the starting point again: how does the unillumined, or unregenerate, human mind find God? How does the human mind, itself a part of the belief that life is material, even glimpse the spiritual? Paul's comment, "The natural man receiveth not the things of the spirit of God,"[1] at least indicates that the problem hasn't changed in two thousand years.

One of the enduring strengths of the Christian Science textbook is that it is a working text. One does not read it once, or even ten times, and then feel he has mastered its contents. It is a book that speaks to many levels of consciousness and sometimes speaks on more than one level itself in the same paragraph. One can muse that the logical male mind would never have written it this way. If that is the case, it is certainly providential that Christian Science came through the intuitions and prayers of a woman. For, as her final testament in writing of what Christian Science is and how it is to be practiced, this book needs to stand the test of time and of changing world outlooks. Four or five generations have now "tested" it. These same generations have experienced the greatest amount of technological and scientific change mankind has seen and the emergence of a nascent global society based on Western organization and the scientific method. Yet, whenever some traditional theological conceptual language still prevails, and even sometimes when it does not, one does not have to read more than a few pages in *Science and Health* to begin to catch the tenor of the message.

That message, however, is interwoven throughout the whole text. The book is theology, practice, motivation, method, all mixed together. One Christian Scientist marked up her copy of the textbook, underlining all the passages she considered to be "absolute" metaphysics—that is, statements about spiritual reality. In a conversation with a practitioner, she mentioned this proudly, as though she now had all the gems of the textbook at her immediate disposal. He smiled at her indulgently, and replied, "Well, now all you have to do is go home and underline the rest, and then you will have it all."

William James, mentioned at length in the first chapter, had an acquaintance with Christian Science that lay somewhere between no understanding of it and a misunderstanding. Yet he admitted the value of Mrs. Eddy's writings in at least one respect. He noted that Protestant theologians had long talked about the need for the individual to pray but that almost no Protestants had the kind of writing that provided them guidance in how to approach God. This he acknowledged had happened with Christian Science.[2]

THE PRACTICE AND PHYSICAL HEALING

After this much prologue, then—what actually is practice in Christian Science?[3]

Practice is prayer, plus putting one's prayers into action so far as possible. Practice is not meditation alone, although what passes for meditation in some religious thinking may be a part of practice in Christian Science also.

Practice involves thinking, but here Mrs. Eddy makes the distinction between the human mind, which, when undirected or undisciplined, is just as often a negative influence, and the divine Mind, or God, whose thoughts are pure and perfect and have the power of enforcing themselves in our experience. "In a world of sin and sensuality hastening to a greater development of power, it is wise earnestly to consider whether it is the human mind or the divine Mind which is influencing one."[4]

Prayer in Christian Science is not primarily one of petition. The all-knowing Mind cannot be petitioned like some medieval king, although the mere act of petitioning may have some benefits. (As one example, it becomes hard to petition a God we believe in for some unworthy purpose or to hide our motives for petitioning.) Prayer involves removing ourselves from the realm of the material senses and entertaining spiritual sense, which does tell us what we need to know of God if we only cultivate it. Thomas Merton, the Jesuit theologian who wrote many moving essays on meditation, makes the point in one of them that we cannot determine to meditate, or at least we cannot determine the outcome of the meditation. Prayer puts us in God's hands, so to speak, and once there we must listen for the intuitions that come from that direction.

While we think of prayer as a kind of mental *action*, part of the activity of prayer involves trying to listen for God's direction. In her own discussion of prayer, Mrs. Eddy begins with a saying of Jesus: "When thou prayest, enter into thy closet, and, when thou hast shut thy door, pray to thy Father which is in secret; and thy Father, which seeth in secret, shall reward thee openly."[5] Then she continues:

> The closet typifies the sanctuary of Spirit, the door of which shuts out sinful sense but lets in Truth, Life, and Love. Closed to error, it is open to Truth, and vice versa. . . . To enter into the heart of prayer, the door of the erring senses must be closed. Lips must be mute and materialism silent, that man may have audience with Spirit, the divine Principle, Love, which destroys all error.[6]

The preparation for practice as prayer, then, is to silence the material senses. If Jesus' saying seems to be interpreted too broadly for some, one need only think of the many times he withdrew himself from his disciples to be alone in prayer.

To whatever degree prayer consists of active verbal statements on the part of the individual, in Christian Science these are mainly statements of metaphysical fact—affirmations of the presence and power of God, of the activity of all his attributes. One identifies himself as God's idea, as an individual expression of Christ, the perfect man, and declares that as this exact reflection he possesses all that he has affirmed as being true of God. He also denies whatever is present in his thought that seems to be doubting the truth of these statements.

One praying in Christian Science accepts the premise that existence is indeed mental. He sees the Christian battleground as one in which two forces oppose each other. On the one side are the forces represented by a selfish, materially minded mentality that believes in a world of good and evil, matter and spirit, divine Providence and bad luck, and a life that has both beginning and ending. On the other side of the field is the force of a wholly benign, all-powerful loving Father-Mother God, who knows no evil and no sets of opposites. Whatever is false when examined in the light of metaphysical fact—that is, whatever part of the belief in a combination of good and evil, or Spirit and matter, has not already yielded to the force and activity of omnipresent good—must give way in the case in question to the spiritual fact.

When I was living in Germany in the postwar years, I developed a sharp pain in my chest over a period of about a week. I was involved in intelligence work for the U.S. Army and operated out of my home most of the time. I was able to keep the discomfort to myself because I rested at home several times during the day. When Sunday came, however, and I could not even remain standing to sing the hymns at the Christian Science church service, I approached an elderly gentleman I knew to be a Christian Science practitioner. I told him the problem, in no more detail than I have just related it here. He said he would be glad to "work" for me, a phrase Christian Scientists use as synonymous with praying. By late afternoon the pain had completely vanished. I had expected it to, of course, but partly out of gratitude and partly out of wanting to see how he would explain the healing I asked if I could come round to his apartment that evening. In the course of the evening, he told me of one of his first healings as a Christian Science practitioner.

"Before the war," he began, "I was living in Berlin. I had a call one evening from a young mother whose small child was critically ill. She asked for help and I said I would pray for the child. As soon as I hung up the telephone, doubts assailed me. What have I promised to do? I thought. Then I began to reason with myself. Here I am in one part of Berlin and there is that lovely young mother with her baby way on the other side of this huge city. What is it that I can do as a Christian Science practitioner? Well, I knew that the only thing I could do was to correct my own thinking about the picture presented to me on the phone, to see that child as the perfect child of God. I also tried to see that young mother as expressing the qualities of God and as such I knew that she could not be fearful for her child. It didn't make any difference that we were physically separated, since we were working in the realm of Spirit, which I knew was everpresent. Yet I was surprised myself when, in little more than an hour, the mother called to say that a marvelous change had already taken place and the child appeared to be all right."

What this practitioner had done was to reject in his own thinking the mental picture that that mother had presented of her child. He had not tried to influence them or hypnotize their thought. But within his own mentality, he had to get it straight what was spiritually true of these two. Any process of mental argument he had briefly employed was for the sole purpose of becoming aware of the presence of the divine Mind. "Remember that the letter and mental argument are only human auxiliaries to aid in bringing thought into accord with the spirit of Truth and Love, which heals the sick and the sinner," says Mrs. Eddy in the textbook.[7] The healing that resulted, as well as the incident of my own already mentioned, gives some indication of the power of a right thought, one that sees as the divine Mind, or God, is seeing, over a false belief. The method needs to be tried, however, to be wholly credible.

Although no two healings are the same, and many are more protracted, the process is similar in each case. The remark is sometimes made that Christian Science is but one more example of the American infatuation with technique. The attempt is made to give all technique a bad name. The Canadian minister, Philip Lee, already quoted in the section on the gnostics, has written an erudite critique of North American Protestantism that contains some valuable insights. Yet he makes this incorrect assumption about technique in Christian Science practice. Naming Christian Science along with several other movements, he says, "Among the various Christian sects and cults that have flourished in America as in no other land ... technique has entirely replaced any genuine concern for God's activity in human affairs."[8]

Technique, one must agree, does not equate with prayer. But it makes a difference whether one thinks of technique as *formula* or as a *method*. In the sense that Mrs. Eddy has given us the broad method of praying—silencing the material senses and entertaining thoughts about God and his perfect spiritual creation—she has given the world a permanent method with which to work. As for the minister's remark that "technique has entirely replaced any genuine concern for God's activity in human affairs," it is precisely God's activity that the practitioner welcomes and expects to see evidence of.

But this criticism helps to highlight the purpose of prayer. For what does one pray? We have said that prayer is primarily not one of petition. If one is praying to see more of God's kingdom on earth, the prayer will usually be specific. But the demonstration the Christian Scientist is making is not one defined by the limits of the material senses—a healthy body, a better job, a bigger house, a kinder husband, or a more generous employer. These may be the things we think we need. On examination, however, a sincere Christian is forced to admit that what he or she really needs, and the only thing he or she needs, is a fuller consciousness of God's presence and power.

A Spiritually Mental Practice

Christian Science practice is a spiritually mental practice, or activity. To some extent, the human mind is involved, although the ideas "it" entertains are neither material nor human in origin. Yet this practice is different in kind from that of the various kinds of psychotherapy that have been developed since Freud, and they too use the mechanism of the human mind. How does one differentiate? What do I mean by the term *spiritually mental?*

In his 1962 book, *The Christian Science Way of Life*, DeWitt John tells a story about Harlow Shapley, a well-known Harvard University astronomer of the time. Prof. Shapley was trying to explain an astronomical concept to the effect that there were outer limits to the universe. A young woman in his class, skeptical of what he was saying, asked, "Suppose I were to go to the very edge of the universe, the limit you speak of, and poke my finger right through?" "Well, I wish you would!" shot back the astronomer. "You see, you are trying to understand a four-dimensional problem with your three-dimensional mind."[9]

Psychologists and some medical people who study the brain are not unanimous in their explanations of the brain's functioning. One can find in the literature much to the effect that, if one thinks of part of the brain's function as a giant computer, the software that tells the brain to master certain problems or think about certain subjects lies somewhere outside the brain itself. Biological research continues to uncover much that we have not known about the brain's functioning, and at least some of it supports Mrs. Eddy's contention that "Mortal mind and body are one."[10]

However, no theory regarding the brain or the relation of an over-all direction of thought to making the brain work out certain problems leads us to spirituality. Trying to define spirituality within the context of the actions of the human mind with which one is familiar is similar to the problem in physics of using the three-dimensional model of the universe to explain the fourth dimension. Perhaps the clearest difference between human intellect and spirituality that I can think of concerns the disconnectedness, the separation, that can occur among so-called thinking individuals and the sense of oneness that is an essential element of spirituality.

As long as one is dealing with the human mind or intellect, he or she is dealing with a sense of separateness, of division between one person and another. Human beings can get along well, of course; they don't always disagree! But we commonly talk about "my" intellect or "your" intelligence. Strangely, or perhaps not so strangely after all, there seems something improper about saying "my spirituality." We would tend to say instead, "She expresses a high degree of spirituality," implying that spirituality itself cannot be divided up or distributed in discrete bits. Whatever differences of meaning human beings have applied to the word *spirit* over the centuries, it has probably always had the sense of a power or presence that, whether expressed temporarily in material things or not, is not itself material—is not limited.

When a Christian Scientist prays, he tries to identify himself with the divine Spirit he calls God. He hopes to realize some of the presence and power of Spirit in the human circumstance that would deny it. To be the most effective, such prayer then proceeds a step farther. The human situation needing healing or correcting is not ignored, but the spiritual thinker tries to see that person, himself or another, or that situation, as the perfect Principle of the universe must see it. He may for a moment or two become literally conscious of nothing else except the activity of this perfect Principle, Love, in holding its expression, man, in its grasp. It is such a moment of spiritual "seeing" that heals. In the words of *Science and Health:* "Become conscious for a single moment that Life and intelligence are purely spiritual,—neither in nor of matter,—and the body will then utter no complaints."[11]

In entertaining that kind of spiritual sense, the individual is not absorbed. There is no loss of individual identity in the practice of Christian Science (as happens in the Western interpretation of some Eastern thought systems). But there is a loss, or fading away, of the material sense definition of man as described by the limits of matter. As the spiritual is seen even in part, the kind of egotism that associates itself with the human mind is one thing that is healed. For, spirituality being universal, it exists for all men to express. In fact, that is how a practitioner is able to heal a patient. As in the case of my friend in Berlin, the practitioner sees both himself and the patient as existing within the orbit of infinite Love.

One might think of God as existing throughout all space, being everywhere, or of himself as existing not in material space or time at all but at that "point" where God is. Joseph Campbell, the late mythologist, wrote of God as a circle whose center is everywhere and whose circumference is nowhere. This is another instance of human language not being entirely adequate to describe the experience of God's presence. But it is this presence that the Christian Scientist prays to realize, and this is the all-important step that makes systematic spiritual healing possible. It also is the key to differentiating the practice of spiritual healing from any other kind of mental activity.

The practice of Christian Science does follow a method, then. But method does not relegate Christian Science to being merely or mainly a technique, and certainly it is not some kind of wishful thinking. Every part of the practice—whether it is to heal a specific claim of sin or sickness or the more general daily practice to replace the limited mortal sense of existence with an increasing sense of the presence, here and now, of the Christ, God's spiritual idea—follows the Christian demand for regeneration. Some part of the old man is being dropped by the recognition of the Christ as each person's real being right now. Perhaps this regenerative aspect of the religion has not been explained well enough in brief discussions of Christian Science. But it is essential to the healing aspect of the religion.

What is being overcome is not only some specific sin, but the entire mortal sense of existence that breeds the specific sins of the fleshly mind. Greed, for instance, which can culminate in crime and violence, arises from the belief that existence is material, that good is limited, that someone else has something we deserve or simply want. It can be recognized as a sinful tendency by any thinking person, but what would be called in Christian Science terminology the Christ, Truth, destroys the false concept by replacing it with an active knowledge that good is spiritual and unlimited. This has to be applied individually in a manner that makes the spiritual reality tangible in each person's experience. Once the presence and activity of the spiritual idea is even partly understood, the foundations of greed are more easily laid aside. This is the case with every sinful tendency. Its destruction comes with the knowledge of what is true in its place.

In one brief discussion, Mrs. Eddy combines this dismantling of error with the truth that frees mankind:

> We cannot fill vessels already full. They must first be emptied. Let us disrobe error. Then, when the winds of God blow, we shall not hug our tatters close about us.
>
> The way to extract error from mortal mind is to pour in truth through flood-tides of Love. Christian perfection is won on no other basis.[12]

The method in Christian Science is not to rehearse the error but, once it is recognized, to cast it out by replacing it with some aspect of the spiritual sense of man—the Christ. The method is simple, so simple in fact that its difficulty is not in the human mind's grasping it but in consistently holding to it. One does not probe the past in Christian Science, as he does in most systems of psychotherapy. The Christian Scientist would hardly deny that the past seems to influence our thoughts and actions. However, Science departs from the method of psychotherapy in its conviction that the entire human sense of existence is in the nature of a dream state when compared to unchanging spiritual reality. Spiritual healing—whether of a physical illness or of a character defect—comes not from digging around in the rubbish of what will eventually be seen as a nonexistent mind, but in adopting the mind of Christ, in living whatever part of spiritual reality one senses through his study and prayer.[13] And in terms of spiritual reality, the belief of a past, as tenacious as it may be, is only another false belief to be laid aside as one better understands the timeless nature of God's beneficence to man.

While the method of practice is drawn out in much greater detail in *Science and Health*, Mrs. Eddy did not think she was going any further than explaining the method Jesus intuitively used. He was so conscious of his sonship with God, of expressing the Christ, that the mental argument most of those who practice Christian Science use was unnecessary.

It is ironic that, in all the discussions of Jesus' Christianity, his healing is either: (1) explained in orthodox Christianity as a unique gift that Jesus possessed as part of the Godhead, (2) seen as a psychic phenomenon unique to him and maybe an occasional other psychic, (3) dismissed as exaggerations similar to those commonly made at the time about other spiritual leaders, or (4) ignored. If one tries to make the religion of Jesus, the religion that he practiced during the three years of his public ministry, the basis of his Christianity instead of the forms and doctrines that grew up during the three centuries immediately after his ministry, it is difficult to see how the healings can be passed over. The synoptic Gospels, in particular, abound in them. There are some twenty-five specific healings, in addition to numerous accounts of his "healing the multitudes."

Many of the specific healings have aspects about them that are strikingly similar to the method of Christian Science practice. For those who have had some experience with the sudden healing of which Christian Science practice is capable, comparisons such as these illustrate the coincidence of elements in Christian Science treatment with Jesus' own practice:

- Jesus' *healing of those who were not physically present.* In the healing of the centurion's servant (Luke 7), the centurion felt he was unworthy to have Jesus come to his house. Noting the centurion's faith, Jesus let him return home, knowing that the healing was accomplished.[14]
- Jesus on more than one occasion *denied the reality of material evidence,* even in the extreme case of apparent death. When he came to heal the young girl who had died,[15] he

allowed only the girl's parents and his own disciples in the
room with the girl. Two points were illustrated in this
case: first, he denied the finality of the material sense evidence, even of death, and second, he could heal more easily if he shut out the merely curious, who in any case
would tend to doubt whether he could bring the girl back
to life.

- Jesus clearly *made no material diagnosis*. He found out on
occasion that someone had been sick for a long time, as in
the story of the man at the pool of Bethesda who had been
ill for thirty-eight years.[16] But he never asked about the
cause of illness or its particular nature. This is clear evidence that what healed was not a knowledge of the material difficulty but a knowledge of the Christ, Truth, which
acts as a law to annihilate whatever claims to enslave man
or deny his perfection.

- Jesus' method was clearly *entirely mental*. He had *no drugs
or surgical methods* at his disposal.

- Jesus could *read the thoughts of others*. He amazed the
Samaritan woman at the well by telling her that her absent
mate was not her husband, and that she had had five hus-
bands before him. Amazed, she could only answer, "Sir, I
perceive that thou art a prophet."[17] Mrs. Eddy explains
this phenomenon thusly in *Science and Health:* "Our
Master read mortal mind on a scientific basic, that of the
omnipresence of Mind. An approximation of this discern-
ment indicates spiritual growth and union with the infinite
capacities of the one Mind." Challenging the growth in
this direction of the individual Christian Scientist, she says
farther on: "We approach God, or Life, in proportion to
our spirituality, our fidelity to Truth and Love; and in that
ratio we know all human need and are able to discern the
thought of the sick and the sinning for the purpose of
healing them."[18]

- Jesus *linked the healing of sickness with the healing of sin*.
When the palsied man came to him for healing, Jesus told

him, "Son, be of good cheer; thy sins be forgiven thee."[19]
This was blasphemous to the Scribes, but indicates that
Jesus very likely discerned that the man's healing was
linked either to his giving up some specific sense of sin (if
so, the Bible does not say what) or perhaps to his giving up
his sense of guilt, the sense that mortal man is by nature
evil and must suffer. Christian Science agrees that the
belief in a mortal man is evil because it is the false sense of
man. That belief must be overcome by the knowledge of
man's innate spirituality and purity.

- Jesus taught the *importance of guarding one's own thinking*.
  Though not an actual healing, the parable of the ten virgins emphasized the need to stand guard over one's
  thought, to be spiritually prepared for coming challenges
  (or even opportunities!) that one might not know how to
  handle without preparation. The five virgins who had no
  oil in their lamps tried to borrow oil from the five whose
  lamps were trimmed, but found their request denied.[20]
  The lesson Christian Science would draw from this is that
  nothing can substitute for the individual spiritual work, or
  prayer, each of us must do if he or she is to be prepared to
  see the kingdom of heaven appear in his or her own life.

- All of Jesus' healing was motivated by his *compassion for
  mankind*. In several references to either his healing or his
  teaching activities, the Gospels begin by saying that Jesus
  was "moved with compassion toward them." It was his
  own life of love, reflecting divine Love, that was the motivation and provided the power for the healing.

These references to the method Jesus employed in his own healing could all be elaborated upon. As has been intimated here repeat-
edly, the method of healing is a rather simple one. The challenge to
practicing Christian Science lies in being consistent and single-
minded. In writing a brief explanation such as this, I have tried to
steer clear of making the practice sound either too simple to be believable or too difficult for the average spiritual thinker to understand.

Some of the wrong concepts about Christian Science, such as that it is concerned with technique or manipulating God to our selfish wishes, may stem from well-intentioned attempts to make the practice of Science intelligible to the casual inquirer. It is intelligible, and it is simple, but it requires the same degree of dedication and devotion that one can imagine from those who enter religious orders to shut out the world from their thoughts. It is, at the same time, the most liberating kind of mental activity known to those who practice it successfully. They come to see increasing evidence of God's law in operation, and to realize that man does exist right now in the kingdom of heaven. In this sense, too, Christian Scientists feel some of the sense of mission and all-engrossing nature of the quest that was typical of the generations of Christians immediately following Jesus.

On this general theme of the difficulty of practicing Science, Mrs. Eddy writes:

> Some individuals assimilate truth more readily than others, but any student, who adheres to the divine rules of Christian Science and imbibes the spirit of Christ, can demonstrate Christian Science, cast out error, heal the sick, and add continually to his store of spiritual understanding, potency, enlightenment, and success. There is nothing difficult nor toilsome in this task, when the way is pointed out; but self-denial, sincerity, Christianity, and persistence alone win the prize, as they usually do in every department of life.[21]

Practice and Christian Regeneration

This discussion of the practice began with a discussion of healing. That is what the average person thinks of first today when he or she hears the words "Christian Science."

But let us now look at the practice in the more general terms in which the word is used in Christian Science. Mrs. Eddy applied this word *practice* to one's whole life as a Christian Scientist. She wrote, for example:

> Every day makes its demands upon us for higher proofs rather
> than professions of Christian power. These proofs consist
> solely in the destruction of sin, sickness, and death by the power
> of Spirit, as Jesus destroyed them. This is an element of
> progress, and progress is the law of God, whose law demands
> of us only what we can certainly fulfill.[22]

And, in spite of her emphasis on spiritual healing as an essential
element of Christianity, she wrote:

> . . . the mission of Christian Science now, as in the time of its ear-
> lier demonstration, is not primarily one of physical healing. Now,
> as then, signs and wonders are wrought in the metaphysical heal-
> ing of physical disease; but these signs are only to demonstrate
> its divine origin,—to attest the reality of the higher mission of
> the Christ-power to take away the sins of the world.[23]

From her own Calvinist background, Mrs. Eddy retained the sense
of making an accounting to God for each day he gave her. The
demonstration of health through spiritual healing provided the
proof she felt was necessary to show that Christian Science was not
her invention but her discovery—and that what she had discovered
was the same system of turning to God that Jesus and, to a lesser
extent, some of the prophets had also used. Much of the language of
the textbook has to do with physical or mental healing, since this was
the element of Christianity that she found missing. However, she
insisted on the regeneration of character as much as would any other
devout Christian. As the years went on, and she found that some of
her early students were themselves more taken with the technique
of mental practice than with living thoroughly Christian lives, this
became the cause of her separation from some of them.

Regeneration in Christian Science has to do both with character
reformation and with changing one's mental base of existence.
Both happen together, or it is best if they do. Dwelling on our sins,
or our shortcomings, is dreary work; even most of the Calvinists eventually thought it too dreary. Changing one's outlook from a material to a spiritual sense of existence, on the other hand, is not
dreary work. It is exciting and even exhilarating.

To aid in this work, Mrs. Eddy established a system of Bible study that, in conjunction with the Christian Science textbook, teaches one how to overcome his or her sins and at the same time to progress out of a limited sense of existence. The overcoming is not drudgery, because progressing out of a limited sense of existence does have for most people the exhilarating sense of a new birth. Most students of Christian Science read the Bible lesson contained in these two books each day—most of them probably read it at the start of their day. In fresh form each week, because the lesson draws from the entire Bible and their six-hundred-page textbook, they find their thought learning about and being drawn into the realm of spiritual reality. Each lesson gives them some new insight into Jesus' example and its relevance to their experience today. God's laws are operative here and now, and the students' study of the lesson gives them fresh thoughts as their basis of departure for the day. Many students attempt to see their entire daily activity as taking place in the spiritual realm. Perhaps instead of thinking of the people they will be dealing with that day, they attempt to see God as expressing his divine will in every activity in which they will be engaged, and to know that as God's child they will individually express intelligence, intuition, compassion for those they meet, and so on.

Such thinking tends to shut out of a person's experience whatever its opposite might be—self-will, egotism, stupidity, dullness, to name the opposites of the qualities just mentioned. The student has to identify himself as well with the Christ, and grow out of any tendencies that would hold back his own progress. Holding on to qualities such as love, kindness, joy, peace is the same kind of spirituality that brings healing of physical ills. Just as some of the less worthy aims that mortals have, such as wealth or peer acceptance, are associated with a limited, material view of individuality, so these other, spiritual, qualities are ones that have no limits and can be shared by all.

Christian Scientists do not keep a diary of their daily mental progress, as some of the early New England settlers did. However, daily study of the lesson-sermon, as well as consistent prayer—even when there is no immediate problem to be worked out—tells us more than we need to know about what steps we need to take to more fully express Christ. In the end, that is what actually defines the practice of Christian Science—expressing the fullness of Christ.

There is a connection between the daily practice of adopting more spiritual qualities as the thoughts one consistently lives with and the healing of physical or mental illness. Mrs. Eddy wrote, "The procuring cause and foundation of all sickness is fear, ignorance, or sin. Disease is always induced by a false sense mentally entertained, not destroyed."[24] One who is practicing Christian Science, either for himself or for others, learns that it is the misconceptions harbored in the consciousness of an individual that need to be corrected in order for there to be a healing. Wrong thoughts manifest themselves in physically inharmonious conditions. These thoughts, of course, may be either conscious or unconscious thoughts. They may be specific, or they may be as general and as unconscious as the universal belief that man is subject to material law and material causation.

As a small example that illustrates this, society today realizes that many physical illnesses result from tension. So there are new kinds of psychological therapy offered to reduce tension or deal with tension. But what really lies behind tension? Is it not usually the belief of limited human mentalities, either rushing against time (another limit) or competing with one another for some limited good? Knowing how to relax physically may be better than staying tense. But a permanent healing would result from seeing that man exists, not in a mortal time frame with only a limited amount of time to get something done, but in the infinite realm of Spirit. He is himself a witness to the unfolding of Spirit's infinite qualities. There is no competition among the individualities created by Spirit, since all of them have the same access to unlimited good. The result of such knowing may not be the same for one's coworkers, even though one has in one sense known a truth that applies to them as well. But the work, or prayer, has been for the individual involved, and he should find a full and permanent release from tension if he handles whatever belief seems to support the tension. One explanation Mrs. Eddy gives of this process of thinking through a situation with the truth about it (the spiritual reality) reads as follows:

> Belief produces the results of belief, and the penalties it affixes
> last so long as the belief and are inseparable from it. The
> remedy consists in probing the trouble to the bottom, in find-
> ing and casting out by denial the error of belief which produces
> a mortal disorder, never honoring erroneous belief with the title
> of law nor yielding obedience to it. Truth, Life, and Love are
> the only legitimate and eternal demands on man, and they are
> spiritual lawgivers, enforcing obedience through divine
> statutes.[25]

The general praying that one engages in makes him more alert to
handle whatever false belief needs correcting when the case involves
physical healing. Fear in some degree almost always needs to be
addressed and overcome. Mrs. Eddy simply referred to John's statement, "Perfect love casteth out fear. He that feareth is not made perfect in love."[26] No such statement as mere words has any more power
to heal, or to break fear in this case, than a magic charm. One must
always get the sense of what is meant; he must apply it to his own
thinking. Some sense of God as Love, as an everpresence that
holds every part of its creation in the palm of God's hand, is needed
to break the fear that somehow man can slip out of God's perfect control.

Most healing involves getting a stronger sense of one's basic identity as spiritual, eternal, perfect, and letting go of the sense of a material body with a mind inside. One statement of Mrs. Eddy's that
supports thinking in this direction is:

> Rightly understood, instead of possessing a sentient, material
> form, man has a sensationless body; and God, the Soul of
> man and of all existence, being perpetual in His own individ-
> uality, harmony, and immortality, imparts and perpetuates
> these qualities in man,—through Mind, not matter.[27]

Each healing one has, or even hears about, tends to support the
emergence of thought from a matter-based creation to one of
divine ideas expressing a limitless, eternal, divine Mind.

So, we have seen a bit about the practice of Christian Science as
it relates to physical healing, and something of the kind of Christian

regeneration that should be going on in the lives of us all and that facilitates the ability to heal when that need arises. This regeneration includes the full gamut of the moral imperatives of the Bible, as well as the need to see oneself in terms of his or her spiritual selfhood, entirely free from a limited, material sense of life.

ENLARGING ONE'S CONCEPT OF THE PRACTICE

There is also a third part of the practice, one that even many Christian Scientists do not take seriously enough. This is the practice that engages the Scientist in the community. The salvation that Jesus demonstrated is individual but does not stop with the individual. Individual salvation, in isolation from concern for others, is actually impossible to attain. Practice, or effective prayer, goes beyond the intellectual or even highest refinements of human intellect to the spiritual. And what is spiritual is inclusive rather than exclusive. We find healing in finding our own concrete being existing in God, who includes us. We find the rest of mankind with us in this spiritual universe, for it excludes no part of God's creation. And this kind of prayer, or practice, is only being obedient to Jesus' second commandment, "Thou shalt love thy neighbor as thyself."[28]

This knowledge has not led Christian Scientists to proselytize others. If Jesus' disciples were not attuned enough to spiritual reality for Jesus to leave them definite instructions, the same can be said of the world at large today. But in a world of more than five billion people, there are millions who yearn for the freedom a true spirituality gives them. Such a spirituality provides this freedom in their present condition, no matter how severe it may be—or how different from the comfortable middle-class environment in which Christian Science is generally known in the United States.

The first place where a Scientist shares his knowledge of the Christ, Truth, is probably in a local branch church. And getting along with others who of necessity are at varying degrees of grasping the radical redirection in their lives that Christian Science both requires and makes possible—that getting along itself can be a lesson in humility, patience, and perseverance.

Another way in which salvation is shared more widely is in using what one thinks he knows of Christian Science to pray for world conditions. Given the destruction that has taken place around the globe in this "civilized" twentieth century, and the numbers of good people who have at least offered public prayers for peace, one might well be skeptical of the ability of any verbalization of thought to change the most destructive tendencies in mankind. Moreover, even if one brings himself to admit that the specific prayer of one person to handle the problems of another does have healing results, it is much more difficult to see how the prayers of the righteous could have stopped a Hitler or a Stalin, a Japanese warlord mentality, the unleashing of nuclear warfare by the United States, and so on. It is certainly easier to see how quiet prayer, together with the action it precipitates first from the pray-er and later from others affected by the prayer, can prevent smaller situations from growing into the crises that seem inevitable once they have occurred.

At the time of the Russo-Japanese War in 1905, Mrs. Eddy requested all Christian Scientists to pray for a just settlement. She was then in her mid-eighties and had for many years lived the life of a lone religious thinker, dealing with the problems of her young and growing church largely by lengthy correspondence with key individuals. She spent many hours of each day alone in prayer.

Within a few weeks of the time she had asked that other Scientists devote specific time to such prayer, President Roosevelt hosted a peace conference for the Japanese and Russians at Portsmouth, New Hampshire, a few miles from Mrs. Eddy's home. It may have been mere coincidence, and Mrs. Eddy herself remarked that it was peculiar for the president to bring the disputants up to New Hampshire.[29] But was it? Was this the unseen hand of God acknowledging one of the powerful forces of spiritual thinking that had affirmed the presence of peace in the midst of war? One does not know, of course. But the experience indicates that Mrs. Eddy clearly foresaw a major role for Christian Science in dealing with world problems from a metaphysical base.

There are many Christian Scientists who do spend consistent time in praying for the world. Many others may not do the mental work of which they are capable, but they are pushing their concept of salvation outward by trying to put into practice the ethical teachings of Christianity as much as possible in their private dealings with others and in the stands they take on public issues. This is particularly effective in the United States, where grass-roots democracy has had a kind of renaissance because of the new communications tools easily available to interest groups. (This has its dark side, also, in a tendency toward single-issue politics, but the possibility of being heard is a strong plus.)

One of the most important ways in which Christian Science engages its students in being aware of the world's needs and praying about them is through the *Christian Science Monitor.* The last major building block in the organizational structure Mrs. Eddy established over roughly the last twenty years of her life was this daily newspaper, founded in 1908. She had already given the trustees of the Christian Science Publishing Society authority to start new publications. Until that date, however, all the publications had been religious magazines, and it would have taken a boldly innovative board of trustees, able to withstand what church members elsewhere might think or understand about the situation, to begin publishing a daily, secular newspaper. At the time she took this step, the losses anticipated from the newspaper during the first year or even longer would deprive the Mother Church of its income from the Publishing Society, on which it was somewhat dependent at the time. She was warned that this would be the case, but told her trustees that they must go ahead at once. "The Cause demands it," she said.[30]

There were multiple reasons for this step. One immediate one was probably her recent experience with the New York press. A vicious lawsuit backed by Joseph Pulitzer attacked her privacy, had as its aim the discrediting of Christian Science, and cost her close to $100,000 (about a tenth of her accumulated financial assets at the time) to defend successfully.[31]

But a more important reason was her realization that Christian Science had an even larger mission in the world than the healing of sickness. That, she said, was only its bugle call to action, the proof that her system was the original Christianity that Jesus had preached. For her, as for many other religious leaders over two thousand years,

BUSINESS REPLY MAIL
FIRST-CLASS MAIL   PERMIT NO 96   PALM COAST FL

POSTAGE WILL BE PAID BY ADDRESSEE

MEMBERSHIP DATA CENTER
SMITHSONIAN INSTITUTION
PO BOX 420309
PALM COAST FL   32142-9143

Visit our website
www.smithsonianmag.com

Smithsonian

SAVINGS CERTIFICATE

Return this card to enjoy the privileges of membership in the Smithsonian Institution, and you'll get **SMITHSONIAN** Magazine for up to 45% off the newsstand price too!

- ☐ 2 years (you get 24 issues) only $52 - **SAVE 45%**
- ☐ 1 year (you get 12 issues) only $36 - **SAVE 25%**

Name: _____

(Please Print)

Address: _____

City: _____ State: _____ Zip: _____

☐ Payment enclosed.   ☐ Please bill me later.

☐ E-mail Address: Please send me email updates and promotions from *Smithsonian* magazine.

6508WD

the main action was in overcoming the sins of the world, in seeing more evidence of the kingdom of heaven active in the affairs of men.

The *Monitor* is read by at least as many non–Christian Scientists as Scientists. Since its expansion in print with a monthly news magazine, *World Monitor*, as well as into radio and television over the past decade, this statement is even truer. The actual numbers of people who receive some version of the *Monitor* today are in the millions each week, the large numbers being due mainly to the *Monitor*'s worldwide shortwave news and religious broadcasting from three locations—Scotts Corners, Maine, broadcasting to Europe and Africa; Cyprus Creek, South Carolina, broadcasting to all of North and South America; and Saipan in the Marianas Islands, broadcasting to Japan, the Asian mainland, Australia and New Zealand, and the islands of the South Pacific.

The purpose of the *Monitor* has not always been well understood. Many Christian Scientists themselves misconceive of it as being mainly a missionary for Christian Science. Through its eight decades of unselfish service in the public interest it certainly has established itself as a very successful missionary. However, it does not appear that Mrs. Eddy saw that as the main goal of her daring venture into daily journalism. The instructions she gave regarding the *Monitor* are slim. She was eighty-seven years old at the time, and while her spiritual lamps were trimmed more than ever, she left the details of how the new venture would be staffed and edited largely to others. What seems to have been most on her mind was at least threefold: first, to establish a standard of honest journalism; second, to coax the thought of Christian Scientists out of a concern with their individual well-being into some acceptance of their responsibility as practicing Christians to take the whole world and its needs into their thought; and, third, to give an example through *Monitor* journalism of the kind of healing influence Christian Science could bring to world affairs.

No thoughtful Christian Scientist thinks that the *Monitor* has wholly succeeded in any of these aims. But the direction has been steady since the beginning—in spite of the many changes in the human management of the paper and in spite of the many face-liftings the product has seen over the years. A few years ago, when there was some fear that the directors of the Mother Church might relinquish the print paper in favor of electronic media, the concern expressed by other media was not feigned. Over the years, *Monitor* coverage has often provided a standard for others; its choice of material to be covered has been watched carefully, and frequently copied.

As for the second aim, many Christian Scientists undoubtedly have a better understanding of and concern for the world than they would have had without the *Monitor*. The daily study of Christian Science, particularly in the kind of highly charged urban society the United States is at the end of this century, requires a major commitment of time from a serious student. It would seem to be easier if that commitment were solely to the study of the Bible, to the metaphysical system of Christian Science, to the working out of what seem to be individual problems. However, just as there is no clear line of demarcation between the kind of regeneration of character that should constantly be taking place and the healing of specific disorders of mind and body, so is there no clear stopping place in thought between the individual and his society. As we advance into the realm of spiritual thinking and discern even partially the connectedness of all life as ideas in the divine Mind, there very naturally comes a deeper concern for involvement in the affairs that go beyond the home or one's immediate community. This involvement may be insufficient, but it is undoubtedly stronger than would have been the case without a daily *Monitor* to encourage the process of widening individual vision.

The effectiveness of such involvement is another matter. Wanting to help a situation is the first step; it is only the first step, however. A Christian Scientist "taking on the world" has the same dilemmas to work out in practice as has anyone else. How can our prayers for peace be most effective? How do we get involved in solving the problem of the homeless in America? How do we get a handle on the related problems of drugs, crime, lack of education, lack of good jobs, and broken families? The *Monitor* is there as a daily reminder that whatever spiritual vision we are developing must be applied to the entire world.

Not all the coverage of the *Monitor* is about problems. The paper also celebrates human achievement, has substantial interest in the arts, and brings some sense of joy and beauty along with each issue (or, in its electronic versions, with each program). In its coverage of the arts, particularly the entertainment arts, the paper's writers and editors have to put into practice their own best sense of the discussion in chapter 2 regarding being in the world but not of the world. To what extent do we celebrate a culture that exhibits a degree of sensuality never before so publicly exalted? Do we screen out what is negative and, in so doing, miss much of the good at the same time? The editors generally find no hard and fast rule here, and the steady flow of mail from the Christian Science subscribers indicates a variety of human judgments about many matters.

As in other expressions of Christianity throughout the centuries, there is generally a conservative and a liberal approach to social matters, or one kind of person who holds fast to the letter and another to the spirit of the religion. This is not an entirely accurate portrayal, perhaps, since the need to make a metaphysically clear statement of Christian Science regarding God and man does give great weight to getting the letter of the religion correct. It is sometimes the case, however, that those who have the letter correct have a tendency to carry over their sense of a spiritually perfect universe into a dislike or intolerance for the gray areas in which so much of human life takes place. (As with the woman taken in adultery whom Jesus in his compassion refused to judge, there still tend to be more judges out there than those who are willing to trust completely to God to make the judgment.) The moral human being, even when his sense of morality is based on an unchanging spiritual standard, is still putting his or her morality into practice in human situations where the answers are not always clear, where he or she may at times be mistaken in judgment, and where one may still on occasion fail to do what he knows is right.

The third part of the *Monitor*'s mission is to be an example itself of Christian Science in practice. While it is not a news organization of advocacy in the narrow sense of the late 1960s, there is one sense in which *Monitor* journalism can be described as advocacy journalism.

Every editor has some vision of the kind of world he would like to see. For an editor who is a Christian Scientist, that world can best be described as the kingdom of heaven. It is a vision of perfection, including the harmonious relationship of all men and nations, which he sees to some extent every time he prays or practices Christian Science.

There is no developed Christian timeline in which the Christian Scientist looks forward to the end of the world or the physical return of Christ Jesus. Rather, he expects that the kingdom of heaven will be seen in varying degrees by individuals for many generations to come. Eventually some may overcome death while still in the flesh, although that is not the concern or a matter of day-to-day discussion among Christian Scientists. Rather, they try to discern God's presence and power in both their individual and their collective activities in practical, tangible ways that advance the human situation out of whatever static or retrogressive condition it is in.

For most writers and editors of the *Monitor*, this has meant in the last generation a concern for the institutions that protect peace by preventing war; a concern for the underprivileged, whether in the free world or the Third World; a concern for the physical environment of the world; greater justice in economic matters. The general outlook of the *Monitor* is moderate and constructive. It may appear at times not critical enough of the powers that be, particularly in the case of American political administrations. The other side of this is that the twentieth century has taught us to be suspicious of all revolutions and to value stability, especially when it is based on constitutional procedures. The *Monitor* is never shrill; the editors work with a strong conviction that God still controls his creation and that their task is to let that fact become more evident in human affairs.

*****

A strong case can be made that there is no such thing as a theoretical Christian Scientist. Christian Science not only includes practice but in one sense *is* practice. We have seen in this chapter that this practice is many-sided. The "point of entry" for many is still often the need of healing. Evidence of the ability to heal is, for most

Scientists, the continuing motivation that, beyond mere human reason, tells them they are practicing a complete Christianity. However, human regeneration—the letting go of both the specific sins common to humanity and the material sense of being itself—remains their constant occupation throughout the cycle of human life. If regeneration in one sense seems complete, if the human character is one that constantly expresses love and the dominion of God over human affairs, there is still the opportunity of drawing closer in thought each day to the divine immanence and demonstrating one's dominion in new situations. Finally, the reaching out to the rest of humanity, not because Christian Scientists are trying to convert it, but because they really have learned to love it, is the need that few have gone far enough yet in fulfilling.

Mrs. Eddy wrote that Jesus established no form or system of worship. Instead, he demonstrated the activity of Life and Love. The only proof one has that he or she is following in the footsteps of the Master is in his or her own demonstration of divine qualities. In that sense, this chapter on practice should be seen as a continuum with the previous one on the theology of Christian Science. For, in the case of Christian Science, a full apprehension of the theology comes only from the practice of what is already understood.

> In order to apprehend more, we must put into practice what we already know. We must recollect that Truth is demonstrable when understood, and that good is not understood until demonstrated.[32]

Chapter 9

An Afterword

In the first chapter of this book I suggested that, just as Christianity itself calls for and provides a sense of being born again, so Christian Science today represents the new birth of Christianity in this age of science. Christianity itself has not changed, but the explication given to the words and life of Jesus by Mary Baker Eddy shows not only its relevance to human need today but how people of what will soon be the third millennium can attain a lifelong guide for their own spiritual growth.

To refer to the discussion of paradigms and paradigm changes in chapter 5, human thought stands in need of a new paradigm—one that accommodates the fact of spiritual healing. Spiritual healing, in turn, will grow as more of human consciousness accepts its possibility. Just as we have seen that physical science often does not see what it is not looking for or is unprepared to recognize, so the reality of the world of spiritual consciousness, governed by unchanging, undeviating spiritual law—implying a supreme Lawgiver—is unknown to the majority of people on earth today. As with Allan Bloom's allusion to the subjects of the great painters of the Renaissance being only so much abstract art to those who are ignorant of the classical and biblical heritage of the West, that which is spiritual lies in the realm of the abstract for all too many today.

To talk about a new model, or paradigm, is not to ignore the differences that exist between a model that admits the presence of spiritual law in what appears to be a material world, and models that apply only to differing perceptions of physical phenomena. For we are not talking simply about a model that operates within human consciousness to make us feel better. We are speaking of spiritual law that operates within the human consciousness, causing a change in its perception *and appearance* of reality *right here and now*. When healing results, there is a change in what appeared to be the commonsense world of material cause and effect. It is beyond the scope of this discussion to even suggest how an ultimate model might look, or how it might be crafted in human language. Nor is that the point here. The point is that, just as new paradigms eventually spring up when there is too much scientific evidence that simply refuses to fit within the confines of the old model, Christian Science through its systematic healing for over one hundred years has established a record that calls for serious attention at the same time that it beckons homeward those who yearn for a pure, simple Christianity.

This discussion has not been filled with testimonies of healing in Christian Science, other than a few examples that attempted to show how the method operates. That record has been well laid out elsewhere—first in *A Century of Christian Science Healing*, published in 1966, and more recently in Robert Peel's book, *Spiritual Healing in a Scientific Age*.[1] The record is also being laid out continuously in published testimonies in the Christian Science periodicals. Over the years that these have been in existence, more than fifty thousand testimonies have been published. Not all of them relate to physical healing, and those that do are not all cases that have been diagnosed first by the medical faculty. However, one cannot read the periodicals—the *Christian Science Journal*, the *Christian Science Sentinel*, and the foreign-language *Christian Science Heralds*—without feeling the deep sincerity that prompts the testifiers to contribute their experiences (which are carefully verified by the editors). In addition, testimonies of physical healing and the solving of myriad other problems through the application of Christian Science are given at over two thousand Christian Science churches at weekly Wednesday evening meetings.

In writing about the healing of sickness, no differentiation was made here between different types of illness. Much of the medical faculty today is willing to accept the effect of thought on so-called psycho-somatic illnesses. The Christian Science record, however, includes every conceivable illness, including the healing of illnesses caused by viruses or germs, the destruction of malignancy and its replacement with normal tissue, and the restoration to proper functioning of organs that had ceased to function correctly or to work at all. This is possible, in the spiritual model Mrs. Eddy laid out, because all being is spiritual and nothing exists that can counter that spiritual fact. "Christian Science heals organic disease as surely as it heals what is called functional," she writes, "for it requires only a fuller understanding of the divine Principle of Christian Science to demonstrate the higher rule."[2] She also included surgery, by which she meant the healing of dislocations or the proper setting and knitting of broken bones, within the possibility of healing, but admonished her students that this branch of healing would be acknowledged last.

This gentle warning indicates her own recognition that men do not come to an understanding of true being all at once. It is up to each person to decide how far he is ready to go with prayer. The fact that Christian Scientists generally do not make use of doctors simply testifies to their satisfaction with spiritual healing. There is also one other factor that is sometimes misunderstood, but within the framework of a discussion about paradigms should be comprehensible. Under most circumstances, a Christian Scientist would not use the services of a professional spiritual healer, that is, a Christian Science practitioner, and of a medical doctor at the same time. In Christian Science one is working first with a change of consciousness. If he or she is working, or praying, from the basis of there being only one reality and that one spiritual, then, at the same time to follow a medical prescription, aimed to doctor a material body, would tend to undermine one's trust in the effectiveness of his or her praying.

The compromises that occur in everyday living are relatively few if one is trying to grow in spiritual understanding. They occur mainly in the area of dentistry and in childbirth. In the latter case, a mother-to-be wants to maintain her own mental dominion over the entire occasion of childbirth but at the same time needs to give adequate consideration to the thoughts and needs that appear to a doctor or midwife she is using. While childbirth is a near-universal experience for younger women, it is an experience that most of them have only a few times. It seems only normal to have someone in attendance for whom it is not a novel experience. (In the United States, almost every state also has a legal requirement for a medical practitioner to be present at childbirth.)

Given the pervasive evidence of spiritual healing that Christian Scientists feel they have, a new paradigm does seem to be in order. For we are dealing here with a set of spiritual rules, or laws, that can benefit every living person. By the nature of spirituality (its inner content, the change of heart, or consciousness, that happens in some degree with every healing), such a model could never be as precisely stated as a mathematical or physical formula. It is not just a cold scientific fact but is inextricably linked to reformation and regeneration of character. It is this fact—that Christian Science demands the same evidence of regeneration that all Christianity calls for—that makes a so-called scientific model difficult to conceptualize. And, for the practicing Christian Scientist, the discussion of such a model is not really very important. But for an inquiring world that wonders where Christian Science "fits in," this concept of a model that recognizes the validity of spiritualized thought *is* called for.

The desirability of including the phenomenon of spiritual healing in the new, or complete, model of Christianity coincides with a parallel development apt to lead to the same end. Over the next decade or two, the popular history of the origins of traditional Christianity is going to be undergoing substantial revision—"popular," because a major part of the task has already been accomplished at the scholarly level. There are at least two related strands of scholarship that will contribute to this revision. First, there has been an increase in the amount of textual criticism and comparison being undertaken in academic institutions. Each new document that is uncovered or translated so as to make it accessible to larger numbers of people adds to our knowledge of the precise time at which the various Gospels were written, which writers contributed to the thought of later writers, even how emerging doctrinal positions influenced the decisions as to which Gospels and Epistles should be considered authentic.

The second strand, or trend, in this scholarship is to apply as many of the standard tests of the historian as possible to what is known of early Christianity and its scriptures. In particular, this involves the cross-fertilization that occurs when the theologian's approach can be combined with that of the historian, the sociologist, and the anthropologist. To take a single example from each discipline: Exactly how did the Romans exercise their control over the hellenized world of the eastern Mediterranean, and particularly over the recently subdued Jewish areas of Judea and Galilee? How did the largely urbanized living patterns of the Jews, scattered over the entire area of the Roman Empire, influence the preaching and spread of early Christianity? And what was the worldview, that is, what were the philosophic assumptions, of those whom the early apostles were trying to reach? Simply to classify the non-Jewish and non-Christian Mediterranean and Middle Eastern world as "pagan" would be to remain ignorant of the influence of Greek philosophy, or Babylonian astrology, or the dualism of the Persians on the thought of those the early Christians were trying to convert.

As institutional and organized Christianity has come down to mankind over two thousand years, it is a combination of many elements:

- the moral and ethical teachings of Jesus;
- the acts, including the physical healings, of Jesus;
- a doctrine *about* Jesus;
- various forms of ecclesiastical structure;
- an accompanying liturgy, usually developed as a close companion to the ecclesiastical structure.

Without claiming that churches do not need structures if they are to be effective operating organizations, I would suggest that the structure of church will come to be understood more in terms of the requirements placed upon it as an organization if it is to fulfill its mission, not as an institution that itself is literally descended from anything that Jesus started. Liturgical practices, likewise, satisfy the elements in human nature that respond to a pattern, to repetition, to group participation, and, yes, to beauty. The repetition of familiar Scripture, or the congregational singing of familiar hymns, is part of virtually every form of Christian worship. But a particular liturgy will also be seen as a temporal response of a particular culture and not as the essential core of the religion.

This will leave those searching for the core of Christianity with the first three elements: the teachings of Jesus, his acts, and the source of the authority with which he both taught and acted. For it was his undoubted authority, at least as acknowledged by his disciples, that accounted for much of the rapid spread of Christianity. As these three elements are more closely studied, it will be seen that a complete Christianity does not exist without the promise of freedom from human ills that Jesus' healings represented, any more than it could exist without obedience to his moral and ethical standards. And the authority for what he said and did will be seen to have had its source in his unsurpassed spirituality, his undeviating sense of his sonship with God. When scholarship reaches this stage, there will be nothing left to separate it from the position that Mrs. Eddy reached through spiritual intuition. With this model, we shall have come home to the core of Christianity.

A model that admits the reality of spiritual phenomena will not be established by fiat or argument. It will become established only as more people recognize the fact of spiritual healing and themselves experience its liberating effects. In his book on scientific revolutions, Thomas Kuhn quotes the German physicist Max Planck:

> . . . a new scientific truth does not triumph by convincing its opponents and making them see the light, but rather because its opponents eventually die, and a new generation grows up that is familiar with it.[3]

* * *

This discussion has not had much to say about Eastern philosophy or religion, or about psychology. Since all these systems are on the rise in the Western world, and particularly in the United States, this is not to overlook them. Just as a Christian Scientist does not mix medicine with a spiritual approach to healing, it is difficult and in fact improvident to mix Christianity with other systems of thought. Each person has to decide what offers him the most in life. Certainly in the West, for a long time, there has been an assumption that Eastern religions are inferior. There is no longer any excuse for an arrogance that was based largely on ignorance. But neither is there any reason to embrace other philosophical or religious structures as allegedly superior when one is largely ignorant of the origins and practice of Christianity that are the base of his own civilization.

To the extent that Christians believe the life of Christ Jesus to have been unique, they would agree with Father Bede Griffiths that the events of his life had meaning for all mankind and will not be repeated. Christianity is only by accident a "Western" religion; it is, in fact, a universal religion. It was the expectation of Mrs. Eddy that her explication of Christianity would in time cover the globe. With her firm hold on a single God, returning Christianity to a pure monotheism, and the evidence of spiritual healing, there is reason to expect that Christian Science will indeed find acceptance by spiritually hungry men and women everywhere. Moreover, the simple church structure that she established (of which next to nothing has been laid out in this book) presents few impediments to the replication of the church in countries all over the globe.

With today's economic thrust of the Orient, particularly Japan, one may assume that Westerners will learn still more about Eastern thought in the next few decades. This is one reason it is so essential to restore the elements of a pure, practicable, healing Christianity— so that Westerners themselves may recover and appreciate again the heritage that has historically been theirs. As small as the Christian Science denomination is today, its students see their religion as being able to meet this challenge for humanity as a whole.

It is obviously easier for those raised in a Western culture to come home to Christianity; it pervades their literature, and much of its idealism is the basis of the goals and actual accomplishments of modern Western societies. The importance of each person, even the concept of guilt (which implies individual responsibility), the equality of all human beings before God—all are concepts that stem from some aspect of the Judeo-Christian tradition. If a new articulation has indeed been given to the religion of Jesus, it is the natural hope of those who follow it to some degree that others will benefit from it as well.

As for psychology, its methods have influenced some part of almost everything we do. Understanding the mechanism of the human mind is helpful in many cases, from child rearing through educational psychology. The Christian Scientist sees the big breakthrough, however, not in knowing the mechanism of the human mind (including its belief in a past that haunts the present reality), but in dropping the belief in a limited, mortal mentality and adopting the spiritual model. These are only words until one has seen the process in action. One of the challenges Christian Scientists themselves face is avoiding practicing Christian Science partly from a sound metaphysical basis and partly from the inheritance most of us have in some degree today of a psychological approach to problem solving. That is the reason for the emphasis in this book on relating Christian Science, as Mrs. Eddy did, only to its biblical origins, and not to similarities or differences that it, and in a broader sense all of Christendom, has with either Oriental thought or psychology.

The manner of the appearing of Christian Science does not seem all that unexpected, when one becomes aware of the nineteenth-century background in New England and of Mrs. Eddy's own preparation through her religious upbringing and her fight against her own illnesses. Yet the fact that Christian Science came, not from someone in one of the academic schools of theology, but from a simple Christian *woman*, was off-putting to both the theologians and the medical people of her day. To some extent that is still the case. Andrew Jackson Davis looked for the millennium to happen in America. Ralph Waldo Emerson looked for the "new Teacher." Yet when Christian Science appeared on their very New England doorstep, not only did neither of them recognize that this might be the awaited event. Neither of them even gave it a serious look. To Christian Scientists, this is no surprise. The three wise men are alleged to have found Jesus in the manger, but none of the theologians of his era recognized that in him the Christ had come.

Whether Christian Science is actually primitive Christianity remains for future generations to decide. Mrs. Eddy referred in particular to the "lost element of healing" that characterized early Christianity. Current biblical studies, along with work done on such newer material as the Dead Sea Scrolls, do not make it that clear what the exact content of early Christianity was. In *Adam, Eve, and the Serpent*, Elaine Pagels says that the new texts have actually made the search for "real Christianity" more difficult. The texts suggest to her "that during the first two centuries the Christian movement may have been more diversified than it is today." Today, she notes, most Christians agree on the content of the New Testament, have a common creed, and more or less similar rituals. "But during the first and second centuries, Christians scattered throughout the world, from Rome to Asia, Africa, Egypt, and Gaul, read and revered quite different traditions, and various groups of Christians perceived Jesus and his message very differently."[4]

Even if there is no agreed definition of what primitive Christianity was, there can be no doubt that Christian Science stands squarely in the mainstream of Jesus' teachings through its emphasis on the uniqueness of his life and works, his lessons dealing with compassion, humility, and a spirituality that separated him from the kingdoms of this world. Those who take up the study of Christian Science almost invariably report the sense of being reborn, of seeing life fresh and new, which characterized the early Christian experience as well.

✳ ✳ ✳

The future of Christian Science, of course, does not rest mainly on some theoretical scientific paradigm that accommodates the fact of spiritual healing. One is inclined to feel, however, that this will be a major step forward. We have seen in the discussion of other scientific discoveries that there can be much good work done within a paradigm by those who follow it but had little or nothing to do with its initial establishment. Much unnecessary damage was done to the Christian tradition by the rather unthinking adoption of scientific rationalism in the nineteenth century. What many thinkers were happy to do was to cast off the parts of Christianity that seemed to stand in contradiction to what they were learning about the origins of the physical universe and man's biological development. This could have been done without casting off the spiritual content of Christianity, and it still will be done as Christian Science is seen for what it is.

However, the main task will remain for Christian Scientists themselves to continue their demonstrations and their "witness," to use a historical Christian term. To do that they have one task that has been added to what the adherents of the main branches of the Christian Church, both Roman Catholic and Protestant, have had to do: they have to run their church themselves. Christian Science is not only the ultimate Protestantism in terms of man's direct, undeviating responsibility for his own salvation. It is also the ultimate form of organization, an entirely nonhierarchical church that can be maintained and sustained only by the love of its members for each other and the world. We have seen how, in an age of empire, the loosely organized churches of the gnostics did not survive. Regardless of the degree to which their doctrine may have swerved from pure Christianity, they came the closest to a "spiritual church" in their era. We have seen how the other churches gradually changed into a hierarchical form with two classes of believers.

The very concept of a church ultimately run by the democracy of its members could probably not have succeeded until democratic forms were more in usage in society as a whole. Today we also know the pitfalls of democracy, but free societies believe that some form of democracy is the best political expression of the moral freedom and responsibility of the individual. In religious matters, a democracy best represents the equality that every person has before God. Within the Christian Science organization, those who conduct church services and run the business affairs of their church are chosen by the members for limited terms of office. All are eligible. It is very easy for a person to go his own way for a while and ignore the needs of the church organization. Most Christian Scientists learn, though, that they themselves might not have their religion without the presence of the church in their community. Service to church is entirely voluntary, however, and therefore the future of the denomination to a large extent does rest on the degree of devotion and love that the members feel for their community—and, ultimately, for the world. While the church's functions are quite simple—basically a Sunday service, Wednesday testimony meeting, a Sunday school, and maintenance of a reading room—the fact that all the work is voluntary and from the membership demands a good deal of effort on the part of active church members.

* * *

A final question needs to be asked: In the spectrum of being in the world but not of it, where does Christian Science actually stand? Are those who think they are practicing Science staying close to the vision Mrs. Eddy had for the religion, or are they practicing an attenuated, acculturated version of what she so painstakingly established during her lifetime?

The answer varies, depending on the individual involved. Even though the denomination has no differentiation into clergy and laity, there are quite naturally many differences in the degree of commitment. There is, however, no point in being a theoretical Christian Scientist; one purchases no social standing or any other kind of admittance ticket in today's world merely by identifying himself with Christian Science. Moreover, since most Christian Scientists are using their religion to work out some specific problem or aspect of their lives at almost any moment, they do have a sense of being committed to their faith.

The question still persists in another form, however. Are the goals they are working toward determined by the Master, Christ Jesus, or by the tone of the society in which they live? In particular, since some four-fifths to nine-tenths of the world's Christian Scientists probably reside in the United States, are the goals and mores of the United States ones they have uncritically accepted? To put the question another way, suppose that four-fifths of the globe's Christian Scientists lived in the United Kingdom, or in France, or in Germany. Would Christian Science have a different tone? To a degree, one would probably have to answer yes. It would be naive to think that any group of people entirely screen themselves off from all the influences around them. Thus, to the extent that Christian Science continues to spread around the world and to have representation from other countries in the ranks of the directors of the church, the other few officials, and in the writers and editors for its periodicals, it will be spared the single-culture syndrome. (This is not to say that identification with everything American is un-Christian. Much of Western society actually mirrors the social and political goals that Christians have had for centuries. It is the uncritical acceptance of an entire ethos that we are saying is dangerous to the practice of Christianity.)

In my own experience, I have noticed some instances where British friends feel that Americans (including some Christian Scientists) are too acquisitive, that our attention is too much on accumulating this world's needs and living up to other people's expectations. This results in some cases in a life that is lived on the edge of personal financial catastrophe and thus with some permanent degree of unnecessary anxiety. But even that American habit is easily excused by the American assumption that tomorrow is always going to be better. No long-term national calamities have yet been seeded in the American psyche. Even today, when some long-term problems such as education and the drug culture are getting too little in the way of real attention, the general American belief is that somehow tomorrow will be better. This optimism acts on the one hand as a hindrance to a seriously crafted solution; but the optimism itself, the concept that tomorrow is open-ended, does serve in another kind of way to ease the path to eventual solutions.

Such optimism of itself is, of course, neither Christianity nor Christian Science. Yet the general belief that tomorrow is not fixed, that the future is open-ended, helps establish a mental environment in which the spiritual insights one receives do have a better opportunity of being implemented. In any case, the concluding pages of a book are not the best place to open up what could be a whole new subject. Acculturation always remains a danger to any religion. As long as a Christian Scientist is seriously trying to follow all the precepts of his religion, this danger of blindly following the mores of the age is minimized—but never entirely absent.

Mrs. Eddy's establishment of the *Christian Science Monitor* is certainly the plainest evidence that she expected her church to stand firmly in the world. As I tried to sketch in the previous chapter, the *Monitor*'s existence as an integral part of Mrs. Eddy's establishment of her church is meant to force on Christian Scientists an awareness of the world's problems and their responsibility to deal with them prayerfully and in any other way of which they are capable. The gnostic concept that salvation is only between an individual and God is blown out of the water by the Christian imperative to practice in the world the ethical demands of Christ Jesus.

A newcomer to Christian Science might, however, find that there is a *tone* to Christian Science that is somewhat different from what he or she has experienced in another Christian church. Although the chapter on practice has indicated the lifelong task we all have of spiritualizing the human consciousness, Mrs. Eddy fully accepted the concept that man is saved *now*. One works out his salvation, the demonstration of his perfection and his oneness with God, only from the basis that that perfect selfhood, the Christ, is already what is true about man. This does not save us from the experiences in which these facts have to be proved; but it is the acceptance of the grace of God that makes the proving possible. One can live with that grace constantly, in trying times as well as buoyant ones.

Many Christian theologians have written about accepting the will of God, about the witness a Christian may have to make even to the point of risking his life for what he knows to be right. A Christian Scientist would not disagree with any of this, but the emphasis in Science is on the dominion that Christ Jesus showed over each challenge. And the emphasis makes a difference. A constant sense of joy can be ours if we consciously feel we are living in God and not in a material body in a hostile, material universe, and that this same God is directing and protecting all our movements. Mrs. Eddy describes this sense in this way:

> The nature of Christianity is peaceful and blessed, but in order to enter into the kingdom, the anchor of hope must be cast beyond the veil of matter into the Shekinah into which Jesus has passed before us; and this advance beyond matter must come

through the joys and triumphs of the righteous as well as through their sorrows and afflictions.[5]

No matter what the challenge, each step we take can be a step back home, to understanding that the Father-Mother will never let man out of his loving care. It is a journey in which the new man, the Christ, is put on to some degree with each step upward, and the path can and should be traveled with lightness of heart, as serious as it is. That, at least, is one meaning I draw from these familiar and comforting words of the Master Christian:

> Come unto me, all ye that labour and are heavy laden, and I will give you rest. Take my yoke upon you, and learn of me; for I am meek and lowly in heart; and ye shall find rest unto your souls. For my yoke is easy, and my burden is light.[6]

NOTES

Chapter 1
WHY RELIGION PERSISTS IN A SCIENTIFIC AGE

1. John 3:6.
2. Allan Bloom, *The Closing of the American Mind* (New York: Simon & Schuster, 1987), 63.
3. Ibid.
4. William James, *The Varieties of Religious Experience*, The Modern Library (New York: Random House, c. 1902), 480–81.
5. Ibid., 484–85.
6. Ibid., 488–89.
7. Ibid., 489.
8. Ibid., 497.
9. John 10:10.
10. Thomas Sheehan, *The First Coming: How the Kingdom of God Became Christianity* (New York: Random House, 1986).

Chapter 2
AMERICANS AND THEIR RELIGIOUS BELIEFS

1. Os Guinness, *The Gravedigger File: Papers on the Subversion of the Modern Church* (Downers Grove, IL: InterVarsity Press, 1983), 56.
2. Ibid., 52.
3. Severin E. Simonsen, *From the Methodist Pulpit into Christian Science* (Sherman Oaks, CA: I. P. Simonsen, 1928), 36–43.
4. Guinness, *Gravedigger File*, 78.
5. Ibid., 103.

6. Kushner, Harold, *Who Needs God* (New York: Summit Books, 1989), 54.

7. George Gallup, Jr., and Jim Castelli, *The People's Religion: American Faith in the 90's* (New York: Macmillan, 1989). Most of the statistics quoted appear in chapters 1 and 2, pp. 3–44.

8. Andrew M. Greeley, *Religious Change in America* (Cambridge: Harvard Univ. Press, 1989), 42–56.

9. Gallup and Castelli, *People's Religion*, 88.

10. Greeley, *Religious Change in America*, 119.

11. Ibid., 121.

12. Dietrich Bonhoeffer, *Sermons on Discipleship* (New York: Macmillan, Paperback, 1963), 103.

13. Gallup and Castelli, *People's Religion*, 90.

14. Greeley, *Religious Change in America*, 47.

15. Gallup and Castelli, *People's Religion*, 3.

16. Ibid., 261.

17. *Christian Science Sentinel*, January 15, 1990, 28.

18. Mary Baker Eddy, *Miscellaneous Writings* (Boston: The First Church of Christ, Scientist, 1896), 21.

19. Ibid., 15.

20. John 18:36.

21. Margaret Miles, "A New Asceticism," *Harvard Divinity School Bulletin* (June/July 1980): 8–9.

22. William Fore, *Television and Religion* (Minneapolis: Augsburg, 1987), 33 ff.

23. John 16:33.

Chapter 3
THE PHYSICAL SCIENCES TODAY

1. Lawrence Leshan and Henry Margenau, *Einstein's Space and Van Gogh's Sky* (New York: Macmillan, 1982), 111.

2. Martin Buber, "What Is Man?" in *Philosophy in the Twentieth Century* (New York: Random House, 1962), 4:695.

3. Ibid., 700.

4. Ibid., 701.

5. Ibid., 718.

6. William James, *The Varieties of Religious Experience*, The Modern Library (New York: Random House, c. 1902, 1927), 120. Emphasis added.

7. Leshan and Margenau, *Einstein's Space*, 26.

8. Ibid., 13.

9. James Burke, *The Day the Universe Changed* (Boston: Little, Brown, 1985), 308.

10. Mary Baker Eddy, *Science and Health with Key to the Scriptures* (Boston: The First Church of Christ, Scientist, 1906), 306.

11. Ibid., 547.

12. Eddy, *Miscellaneous Writings* (Boston: The First Church of Christ, Scientist, 1896), vii.

13. Eddy, *Science and Health*, 478.

14. Ibid., 328.

15. Adolf von Harnack, "The Essence of Christianity," in *The World Treasury of Modern Religious Thought*, ed. by Jaroslav Pelikan (Boston: Little, Brown, 1990), 378.

Chapter 4
THE EARLY CHURCH

1. W. H. C. Frend, *The Rise of Christianity* (Philadelphia: Fortress, 1984), 42.

2. Edward Gibbon, *The Decline and Fall of the Roman Empire* (abridged ed., D. M. Low, editor) (New York: Harcourt, Brace, 1960), 181.

3. Ibid., 165.

4. Henry Chadwick, *The Early Church* (Baltimore: Penguin Books, 1967), 72.

5. Ibid., 55.

6. Gibbon, *Decline and Fall*, 161.

7. Ramsay MacMullen, *Christianizing the Roman Empire* (New Haven: Yale Univ. Press, 1984).

8. Gibbon, *Decline and Fall*, 172.

9. Jaroslav Pelikan, *The Christian Tradition: A History of the Development of Doctrine, vol. 1, The Emergence of the Catholic Tradition (100–600)* (Chicago: Univ. of Chicago Press, 1971).

10. Ibid., 131.

11. Ibid.

12. Chadwick, *The Early Church*, 76.

13. Pelikan, *Catholic Tradition*, 145.

14. Ibid.

15. Ibid., 149.

16. Ibid., 155.

17. I Cor. 15:19.

18. Pelikan, *Catholic Tradition*, 154.

19. Ibid., 155.

20. Ibid.

21. Chadwick, *The Early Church*, 101.

22. Ibid.

23. Ibid., 31.

24. Will Durant, *The Story of Civilization, vol. 3, Caesar and Christ* (New York: Simon & Schuster, 1944), 672.

25. Renée Weber, *Dialogues with Scientists and Sages: The Search for Unity* (London: Routledge & Kegan Paul, 1986), 162.

26. Quoted by Elaine Pagels, *The Gnostic Gospels* (New York: Random House, 1979), xxxi.

27. Helmut Koester, *Ancient Christian Gospels* (Philadelphia: Trinity Press International, 1990), 50.

28. Psalm 46:6.

29. Luke 12:15.

30. Galatians 5:22, 23.

31. Philip J. Lee, *Against the Protestant Gnostics* (New York: Oxford Univ. Press, 1987), 17.

32. Pagels, *The Gnostic Gospels*, 101.

33. Ibid., 144. See also "The Gospel of Truth," published in *The Nag Hammadi Library*, rev. ed., James M. Robinson, editor (San Francisco: HarperCollins, Paperback, 1990), 40.

34. Pagels, *The Gnostic Gospels*, 144.

35. Ibid., 145.

36. Elaine Pagels, *Adam, Eve, and the Serpent* (New York: Random House, 1989), 18–20, 85–87.

37. Lee, *Against the Protestant Gnostics*, 23.

38. Johann Wolfgang von Goethe, *Faust* (New York: Knopf, 1963), I:1112–17.

39. John 3: 6, 7.

40. Pagels, *The Gnostic Gospels*, 144.

41. John 8:32.

42. Pagels, *The Gnostic Gospels*, 144.

43. Lee, *Against the Protestant Gnostics*, 28.

44. Matthew 18:20.

45. Lee, *Against the Protestant Gnostics*, 28.

46. Laurens Van der Post, *Jung and the Story of Our Time* (New York: Random House, 1977 (orig. 1975), 188–89.

47. Pagels, *The Gnostic Gospels*, 147.

48. Ibid., 102. For exact text, see "Second Treatise of the Great Seth," *The Nag Hammadi Library*, 366–67.

49. Pagels, *The Gnostic Gospels*, 106.

50. Ibid., 108.

51. Lee, *Against the Protestant Gnostics*, 33.

52. Chadwick, *The Early Church*, 285.

53. Mary Baker Eddy, *Science and Health with Key to the Scriptures* (Boston: The First Church of Christ, Scientist, 1906), 238.

Chapter 5
THE NATURE OF DISCOVERY

1. Richard Bergland, *The Fabric of Mind* (New York: Viking Penguin, 1985), 9.
2. Thomas S. Kuhn, *The Structure of Scientific Revolutions*, vol. 2, no. 2, *International Encyclopedia of Unified Science* (Chicago: Univ. of Chicago Press, 1962), 11, 92.
3. Bergland, *The Fabric of Mind*. See chapters 10 and 11, pp. 83–109.
4. Ibid., 44.
5. Ibid., 45–46.
6. Robert Weisberg, *Creativity: Genius and Other Myths* (New York: W. H. Freeman, 1986).
7. Ibid., 14.
8. Ibid., 145.
9. Timothy Ferris, *Coming of Age in the Milky Way* (New York: Anchor Books, 1989), 79.
10. Ibid., 116.
11. Habakkuk 1:13.

Chapter 6
THE NINETEENTH-CENTURY BACKGROUND

1. Perry Miller and Thomas H. Johnson, *The Puritans* (New York: American Book Co., 1938), 60.
2. Ibid., 43.
3. Perry Miller, *Errand into the Wilderness* (Cambridge: Harvard Univ. Press, Belknap Press, 1956), 93.
4. Ibid., 51.
5. Ibid., 82.
6. Miller and Johnson, *The Puritans*, 55.
7. Ibid., 11–12.
8. Ibid., 61.
9. James Michener, *Chesapeake* (New York: Random House, 1978), 412–13.
10. Octavius B. Frothingham, *Transcendentalism in New England* (New York: Putnam, 1876), 355.
11. Ralph Waldo Emerson, *The Best of Ralph Waldo Emerson*, Classics Club Edition (Roslyn, N.Y.: Walter J. Black, Inc., 1941).
12. Arthur Wrobel, ed., *Pseudo-Science & Society in 19th-Century America* (Lexington: Univ. Press of Kentucky, 1987), 74 ff.
13. Ibid., 80.
14. Ibid.

15. Ibid., 166.
16. Ibid., 166–77.
17. Ibid., 100.
18. Ibid., 110.
19. Ibid., 117.
20. Ibid., 115.
21. Ibid., 215.
22. Ibid., 219–20.
23. Archives of The Mother Church, The First Church of Christ, Scientist.
24. Archives of The Mother Church; photostatic copies of Quimby papers in the Library of Congress.
25. Archives of The Mother Church; letter dated March 2, 1866.

Chapter 7
THE METAPHYSICS OF CHRISTIAN SCIENCE

1. Mary Baker Eddy, *Message to The Mother Church for 1900*, (Boston: The First Church of Christ, Scientist, 1900), 2.
2. Mary Baker Eddy, *Science and Health with Key to the Scriptures* (Boston: The First Church of Christ, Scientist, 1906), 587.
3. Deuteronomy 4:39.
4. Romans 8:7.
5. Psalms 139:7.
6. Deuteronomy 32:4.
7. John 18:38.
8. Eddy, *No and Yes* (Boston: The First Church of Christ, Scientist, 1908), 19.
9. Ibid., 20.
10. Eddy, *Science and Health*, 213.
11. Northrop Frye, *The Great Code: The Bible and Literature* (New York: Harcourt Brace Jovanovich, 1983), 17.
12. Ephesians 4:13.
13. Eddy, *Science and Health*, 258.
14. Ibid., 295.
15. Ibid., 119.
16. Jaroslav Pelikan, *The Christian Tradition: A History of the Development of Doctrine, vol. 1, The Emergence of the Catholic Tradition (100–600)* (Chicago: Univ. of Chicago Press, 1971), 36.
17. Eddy, *Science and Health*, 269–70.
18. Mary Baker Eddy, *Rudimental Divine Science* (Boston: The First Church of Christ, Scientist, 1908), 6.
19. 2 Corinthians 5:1.
20. Eddy, *Science and Health*, 484.

21. Ibid., 334.
22. Ibid., 497.
23. Ibid., 533.
24. Renée Weber, *Dialogues with Scientists and Sages: The Search for Unity* (London: Routledge & Kegan Paul, 1986), 174–5.
25. John 8:58.
26. Weber, *Dialogues with Scientists and Sages*, 174.
27. Eddy, *Science and Health*, 295.
28. Pelikan, *Catholic Tradition*, 152. Emphasis added.
29. Eddy, *Science and Health*, 115–16.

Chapter 8
THE PRACTICE OF CHRISTIAN SCIENCE

1. 1 Corinthians 2:14
2. William James, *The Varieties of Religious Experience*, The Modern Library (New York: Random House, c. 1902,1927), 397. Although not specifically naming Christian Science in this reference, James included it in his discussion of what he called "mind-cure" systems in Lectures IV and V.
3. No single discussion of Christian Science practice can do more than introduce the subject. Even in "Recapitulation," the chapter in *Science and Health with Key to the Scriptures* that is used as the basis for class instruction in Christian Science, Mrs. Eddy answers the question, "Will you explain sickness and show how it is to be healed?" by referring the reader to the chapter in the textbook called "Christian Science Practice" (p. 495).
4. Eddy, *Science and Health*, 82–3.
5. Matthew 6:6.
6. Eddy, *Science and Health*, 15.
7. Ibid., 454–55.
8. Philip Lee, *Against the Protestant Gnostics* (New York: Oxford Univ. Press, 1987), 110.
9. DeWitt John,*The Christian Science Way of Life* (Boston: The Christian Science Publishing Society, 1962), 53.
10. Eddy, *Science and Health*, 177.
11. Ibid., 12.
12. Ibid., 201.
13. The contents of the "mind of Christ" are suggested by two verses from Philippians: 2:5, "Let this mind be in you, which was also in Christ Jesus," and 4:8, "Finally, brethren, whatsoever things are true, whatsoever things are honest, whatsoever things are just, whatsoever things are pure, whatsoever things are lovely, whatsoever things are of good report; if there by any virtue, and if there by any praise, think on these things."

14. This method of healing, which is common in Christian Science, is sometimes casually but incorrectly referred to as "absent treatment." It is based on
the metaphysical fact that Mind, God, being everywhere present, the consciousness of both practitioner and patient exist in this Mind and are thus not
separated from each other. In *Science and Health*, Mrs. Eddy writes: "Science
can heal the sick, who are absent from their healers, as well as those present,
since space is no obstacle to Mind." (p. 179).
15. Luke 8: 41, 42, 49–56.
16. John 5:2–9.
17. John 4:19.
18. Eddy, *Science and Health*, 95.
19. Matthew 9:2.
20. Matthew 25:1–13.
21. Eddy, *Science and Health*, 462.
22. Ibid., 233.
23. Ibid., 150.
24. Ibid., 411.
25. Ibid., 411.
26. 1 John 4:18.
27. Eddy, *Science and Health*, 280.
28. Matthew 19:19.
29. Archives of The Mother Church, L06991, September 4, 1905.
30. Ibid., L00593, September 3, 1908.
31. Ibid., L09788, May 17, 1907; L13413, January 10, 1908; and L14015, March
10, 1909.
32. Eddy, *Science and Health*, 323.

Chapter 9
AN AFTERWORD

1. Robert Peel, *Spiritual Healing in a Scientific Age* (San Francisco: Harper &
Row, 1987).
2. Eddy, *Science and Health*, 162.
3. Thomas S. Kuhn, *The Structure of Scientific Revolutions, vol. 2, no. 2,
International Encyclopedia of Unified Science* (Chicago: Univ. of Chicago Press,
1962), 151.
4. Elaine Pagels, *Adam, Eve, and the Serpent* (New York: Random House, 1989),
151–52.
5. Eddy, *Science and Health*, 40–1.
6. Matthew 11:28–30.